Small Medium at Large

How to Develop a Powerful Verbal Sense of Humor

D1399657

Paul E. McGhee, Ph.D.

ISBN: 1-4107-0153-0 (e-book)
ISBN: 1-4107-0154-9 (Paperback)

This book is printed on acid free paper.

1stBooks – rev.12/18/03

Contents

Introduction

"The most completely lost of all days is the one on which we have not laughed." (French proverb)

Have you ever wondered why the endless jokes you've heard and read over the years never nurtured your ability to create your own humor? The reason is that just hearing or reading a joke gives you no opportunity to extend your own comedic creativity. It gives you no chance to exercise your own ability to come up with something that would make it funny.

We are generally presented with the entire joke on a silver platter. Even as kids, we rarely came up with our own riddles (the ones we did create weren't funny). We just faithfully told the ones we heard from others. If you've had children of your own, you know that many of the same jokes you heard as a kid are still circulating today.

This book will help you start thinking like a comedy writer or humorist. It provides over 350 opportunities to stretch your humor skills, giving you practical experience at doing what a joke writer does when writing new material.

We all love to be around people who make us laugh. At parties and other social occasions, those who are gifted in telling jokes and stories or creating spontaneous witticisms invariably have a crowd around them. At some point in your life, you've probably found yourself thinking, "Boy, I wish I could do that." In comparison to their skills, you feel humor impaired.

If you're like most people, you assume you're either born with a good sense of humor, or you're not. And if you're not, you're automatically relegated to the camp of those who can only enjoy the jokes, stories, and spontaneous wit of others. What you don't realize is that witty people and great joke tellers have been working at it most of their lives. They've had a lot of practice! You, on the other hand, probably have never made an effort to improve your ability to remember jokes and stories or create your own spontaneous humor.

Chances are that you're not humor impaired, and that you love humor—which is probably why you bought this book. So rest assured that even people with a good sense of humor will benefit from working with these jokes in the manner I suggest below.

How This Book Will Improve Your Ability to Create Humor

This book will help improve your ability to create original humor spontaneously by giving you repeated opportunities to come up with your own funny lines. The most important feature of the book is that it does most—but not all—of the work for you by setting up a context in which everything is provided except a key word or phrase that completes the punch line. You provide the punch line. A clue is provided to help you focus your thoughts in the right direction. Once you've made the effort to come up with your own answer, you can check the answer given at the end of that section.

The reason this approach works is that it calls attention to the different types of thinking that are involved in the creation of a joke. In the seminars I provide on humor and stress to organizations around the country, a common complaint is, "I just can't think of anything funny to say. No matter how hard I try, I just can't think that way." By the time you become an adult, you've had years of practice at thinking in a "straight" direction. To create humor, you've got to learn to think "crooked." You have to learn to play with words and ideas. You need experience at exaggeration, understatement, reversal, and other traditional techniques of making up jokes.

When we were children, we all loved to play. We could spend all day playing. Most of this play was physical, but as we got older we learned that playing with ideas was fun too. We all went through the "riddle stage," during which we drove our parents crazy with endless riddles. We found great pleasure in turning the world upside down by distorting things, exaggerating, saying the opposite of what we really meant, and so forth. In order for you to become skilled at creating your own verbal humor now, you need to rediscover that child-like enjoyment of playing with ideas. This book will help you achieve this by getting you actively involved in the process of creating humor.

How Do Humorists Think?

How do people (like Steve Allen, Jerry Seinfeld or Eddy Murphy) who are good at coming up with original verbal humor think? They think the way we all thought when we were kids. They love to play with ideas—to distort things, or twist them around. They're very flexible mentally, and are much more willing than the rest of us to consider crazy ideas "just to see what happens." They're good at spotting life's absurdities, ironies, and incongruities. They see the ridiculous side of everyday situations that the rest of us take for granted or don't notice at all.

I argued in my 1979 book, *Humor: Its Origin and Development* (now out of print) that humor is basically play with ideas. A humorist is just a big kid who never stopped playing. S/he just switched from playing physically to playing mentally. And when it comes to playing with ideas, there's no limit! The entire world of everyday experience is a potential playground.

Humorists especially love to play with language. Language, after all, is our main vehicle for thinking about the world. And while language is not essential to humor, it plays a key role in the humor of most of our everyday social interactions. Think back to the time (around first grade) that you first realized that words could have more than one meaning. Do you remember how exciting it was to trick someone else in telling riddles? If you come from my generation, you'll recall such groaners as "Why did the moron bury his car?" "Because the engine died." Or, still worse, "Why did the moron jump off the Empire State

Building?" "Because he wanted to try out his new spring suit."

This kind of humor, of course, is known as a pun. The reason we groan at puns as adults is precisely because they're generally very simple. Basically, puns are children's humor. And yet this is the level at which you probably stopped developing your own humor skills.

Many of us couldn't come up with a spontaneous pun or other funny remark in the next 10 minutes of conversation if our life depended on it. The 1940's comic Jack Benny, however, had a wonderfully funny response when, in a skit, a mugger came up to him and shouted, "OK, buddy, your money or your life!" Benny hesitated, and hesitated even longer, and finally the mugger repeated, "I said, your money or your life!" Benny responded, "I'm thinking it over." (Jack Benny was known to be very "tight" with his money.)

This book develops your ability to create verbal humor by starting with puns, and then sampling a broad range of other joking techniques. With practice, your ability to see the potential for humor in everyday language will quickly grow.

The Nature of Puns

A pun is a play on words that have the same (or similar) sound, but different meanings. The essential ingredient in all puns is ambiguity of the meaning. Many words have more than one meaning, but the context makes the appropriate meaning clear. In riddles and jokes based on puns, we are led to adopt a meaning that makes no sense, or is absurd, in the context set up by the joke. In some cases, the word is spelled the same way for both meanings. Consider the following joke:

A woman calls her doctor and says, "Doctor! Doctor! I just swallowed a spoon, what should I do?" The doctor says, "Sit down and don't stir!"

The key word, obviously, is "stir." We get the joke and see the humor in it when we identify the second meaning. The phrase "Sit down and don't stir" normally means to not move around. In this case, though, given that she's swallowed a spoon, the second meaning is technically possible. But the silliness or absurdity of the idea of using a spoon in the stomach to stir like you would stir something in a bowl makes it funny.

In other cases, puns are based on very different types of ambiguity. For example, we could build jokes around words that are spelled differently, but sound the same (pear/pare/pair). Linguists point out many other ways in which we play with the sound and meaning of words. We will not discuss these here, but you will note many different types of puns throughout this book. Knowing the academic distinctions made between different puns (e.g., homographic or homophonic) is not essential to learning to develop this part of your sense of humor. A linguistic analysis of word play in terms of phonology, morphology, semantics, syntax, and pragmatics is not needed to learn how to think of funny lines. The key to becoming a skilled punster or spontaneous wit is best summed up by the well-known story of the teenager who asked someone on the streets of New York how to get to Carnegie Hall. The answer was, "Practice, practice, practice." This book gives you that practice.

Learn to Look for Ambiguity

To benefit the most from this book, you should use it not only as a means of exercising your ability to create humor, but as a reminder to be on the lookout for verbal ambiguity in everyday life. The most important lesson to learn at the start is that everyday language is full of ambiguity. We aren't aware of it as a rule, because the context makes the intended meaning clear. But that doesn't rule out the possibility of other meanings. You want to establish the habit of becoming aware of ambiguity, regardless of whether or not it's funny. This is an important preliminary step to learning to create your own humor based on ambiguity.

The most effective way to establish the habit of detecting ambiguity is to put it on the "front burner" for a few weeks. Carry a notebook around with you and be on the look out for double meanings and ambiguous words or phrases everywhere you go. This will take a conscious effort at first, but you'll soon find yourself noticing them automatically, with no effort at all.

As a preliminary test, consider the sentences below. These are not jokes, but they all contain ambiguity. Determine for yourself how quickly you see the ambiguity. Sentences like these are written and spoken every day. Actively listen and look for them over a period of several weeks. When you get to the point that you perceive them easily and automatically, you will have taken a major step toward building an outstanding verbal sense of humor.

He went deer hunting with a club.
He helped the woman with the hat.
The men all laughed at work.
The restaurant stops serving crabs after 9:30.
The fat politician's wife loves chocolate.
The shooting of the thieves was terrible.
   (Find at least three meanings here.)
The turkey is ready to eat.
The mayor asked the police stop drinking while
   driving.

If you make a habit of looking for this kind of ambiguity in conversations, newspaper headlines, signs and bumper stickers (even when no one is trying to be funny), you'll find that it will strengthen your ability to guess the punch lines in this book. It will also quickly accelerate your ability to come up with your own spontaneous puns and other types of verbal humor.

Newspapers now commonly include play with words in headlines. Here are a few examples:

Grandmother of 14 shoots hole in one.
Searchers find Big Ugly child (from a Big Ugly,
   W.Va. newspaper).
Ban on nude dancing on Governor's desk.
Furniture drive for homeless launched.

You will also find word play in ads. One ad said:

Braille dictionary for sale. Must see to appreciate.

Even businesses are getting into the act (sometimes unintentionally).

Six muffins for $1.50. Limit three per customer.
Ask about our layaway plan (in a funeral parlor).
Ears pierced while you wait.
Use stairs for restroom.
Please wash hands before resuming work (in a state
    unemployment agency—which also has a
    cafeteria).
Twenty-five years at the same spot (in front of a
    dry cleaning establishment).
Husband exterminators and pest control. (The
    business is owned by a family named
    "Husband.")

An excellent exercise to do whenever you have a spare moment (when stuck in traffic, waiting in grocery lines, sitting through a dull meeting, etc.) is to take any word that comes to mind and think of as many meanings as you can for that word. Do this with a partner whenever possible, since your partner will think of meanings you don't think of, and this will further trigger associations of your own in unexpected directions. Whenever possible, write them down as you think of them. The more you do this, the more rapidly you will acquire the habit of thinking of extra, unintended meanings of words without really trying.

These strategies are discussed in detail in my book, *Health, Healing and the Amuse System: Humor as*

Survival Training. That book provides a ready-made program for gradually improving your sense of humor so that you can use it to cope with the common stresses of everyday life. One part of this program focuses on the development of verbal humor skills, but the overall goal of the program is to improve all the basic parts of your sense of humor, including finding humor in everyday life, laughing at yourself, and using or finding humor in the midst of stress.

Types of Verbal Humor

All humor experts have their own way of classifying types of humor. The problem is that any given joke can be classified in several different ways. The following jokes are examples of just a few commonly-used classifications.

1) Jokes Based on Word Combinations

A drug company has come up with a new drug. It's half decongestant antihistamine and half tranquilizer Methodone. They're calling it "Methodist."

2) Cross Jokes

What do you get when you cross a turkey with a centipede? Drumsticks for everybody.

What do you get when you cross a birth control pill with LSD? A trip without the kids.

3) Daffynitions

What do you call a knife that cuts four loaves of bread at the same time? A four loaf cleaver.

Defeat: De parts of de body dat are connected to de legs.

4) Differences

What's the difference between the USA and Russia, Poland, Romania, and Czechoslovakia? The USA has a Communist Party. (A joke told following the break-up of the Soviet Union.)

5) Exaggeration

Our plane waited on the runway so long they allowed conjugal visits.

The rain here in Los Angeles has caused a lot of mudslides. I was on my way to work the other day, glanced out the window, and my house was making better time than I was.

6) Light Bulb

How many _____ (fill in your favorite target or victim) does it take to change a light bulb?
Four, one to hold the bulb, and three to turn the ladder.

7) Nonsense

A five-year-old asks his mother if he can watch the solar eclipse. "OK," she says, "but don't stand too close."

8) Reversals

He's so rich that when he writes a check, the bank bounces.

9) Substitution of a Similar-Sounding Word

I was such a great lover on my honeymoon that my wife gave me a standing ovulation.

These jokes could have been classified in more than one way, but this gives you a taste of the kinds of classifications typically used. In this book, the choice has been made to simply allow the reader to learn by repeated example. Rather than asking you to think about what kind of technique is used for a joke, you are asked to focus on finding a funny answer—regardless of the nature of the technique. As you go through example after example, you will begin to find funny punch lines occurring to you without ever giving a thought to the kind of technique that would work best.

This is the kind of practice that will serve you best in everyday life. You want to get to the point that puns and other forms of play with language just pop into mind without any effort on your part. However, some readers will find that they make more rapid progress in improving their joking skills by asking, "OK, what's going on here? Why is this funny?" In doing this, you will generate your own categories as you go. But if you are someone who finds that this makes work out of something that should be fun, you should by all means avoid any effort to actively question why it's funny or to generate your own categories.

Many of the jokes and stories included in this book could be put into two or more of the categories listed above. I initially planned to have separate sections of the book devoted only to examples of a particular type of humor. It became obvious, however, that this not only makes the jokes and stories repetitious and less fun; it also prevents you from having the opportunity to make your own judgment of what kind of punch line is called for in each case. Your humor skills will develop more rapidly by working with the different techniques in a relatively random order.

Organization of the Book

The initial collection of puns, signs, children's confusion, headlines, and oxymorons is designed to give you experience at guessing the answers to easier forms of humor. But even puns are not easy to guess without clues. A broad range of difficulty is provided throughout the book, so you can expect some successes and some failures.

How to Use This Book

To benefit the most from this book, you must resist the temptation to simply look up the punch line at the end of that section. Cover up the clue that follows the joke, and give yourself 30 seconds to come up with some kind of joking answer. Then check the clue. If you come up with an answer without looking at the clue, the clue will either confirm what you were thinking, or point you in some new direction. If you fail to come up with an answer, the mental effort you've made will still help you improve your humor skills (especially if you do this throughout the book). After reading the clue, give yourself another 30 seconds to come up with an answer before checking the one given in the book.

You will know that your ability to "think funny" is growing when you gradually get better at coming up with your own funny answers. These may or may not match the answers provided. But you should not consider your answer wrong if it differs from the one given here. Many jokes and stories can be completed in more than one way and still be funny. And remember, there are no absolutes when it comes to what is funny. If it's funny to you or someone else, then it's funny! Don't worry about it if your sense of humor fails to match someone else's.

Be sure to fight the temptation to simply look up the missing part of the punch line without making an effort to think of a funny line yourself. You can go through the entire book this way and have a lot of fun, but you won't improve your humor skills. You'll be no better at creating your own humor after finishing the book than you were before you started it. Improvement will come only if you struggle a bit with each example.

If you adopt the habit of looking up the answer without trying to think of one yourself, you rob yourself of your best opportunity to gain from the book. Once you have seen the answer given, it is no longer possible to stretch your own humor skills. As you read the jokes the second time, you'll automatically be drawn toward trying to remember the answer you saw the first time. As you gain more experience with the many kinds of humor represented in the book, you will gradually find funny answers popping into your mind with less and less effort.

You will discover that trying to think of funny punch lines is mentally tiring at first. So don't try to read the entire book at one sitting. Put it in a place where you can spend 15-30 minutes with it before going on to something else. Otherwise, you'll fall into the habit of just looking up the answer without trying to think of one yourself.

Once you have finished the book, let it sit for a month or more, and then come back to it and go through all the examples again. You will remember many of the answers, but going through the motions of generating the answer again—even from memory— will help consolidate the gains toward thinking like a humorist that you made the first time through the book.

Puns

1) A handsome young man invited his beautiful Chinese date up to his apartment to see his stamp collection as they left the movie theater. He told her he found her very attractive, intelligent, and talented. The girl smiled, shook her head "no," and said, "_____ will get you nowhere."
Clue: Think of the familiar phrase women use when reacting to a compliment. Also, what is the name given to stamp collecting? The fact that she's Chinese adds a little something extra.

2) A psychiatrist who strongly believes in the notion of a "collective unconscious" complains that he always has trouble getting served in bars. "All the bartenders say I'm just too _____."
Clue: What early follower of Freud believed in a collective unconscious? His first name is Karl.

3) Sign in front of a Body and Fender Repair Shop: "May we have the next _____?"
Clue: Play with a formerly familiar phrase from ballrooms.

4) When the nudist colony opened just outside town, everyone expected a great deal of media attention, but there was very little _____.
Clue: A familiar word used by the mass media.

5) An elephant in the jungle was drinking at the edge of a river when he spotted a snapping turtle asleep on a log. He ambled over and kicked it all the way across the river. "Why did you do that?" asked a giraffe standing nearby.

"Because," said the elephant, "I recognized it as the same turtle that took a nip at my trunk 20 years ago."

"What a memory!" said the giraffe, in admiration.

"Yes, being an elephant, I have _____ recall."
Clue: They say an elephant never forgets. Play with the sound of the word that goes before "recall."

6) Show me a metal worker who knows how to make the hardware for bathrooms, and I'll show you a man who knows how to forge_____.
Clue: Make progress.

7) What kind of people are retread tires made for?
  People who are old enough to _____.
Clue: What do people generally do when they get to their middle sixties?

8) When Europeans first discovered how to make expresso coffee, everyone was very excited about the stimulating new taste. All agreed that this gave them _____ for a big celebration.
Clue: What term is used to refer to the by-product of making coffee?

9) A lady caused a big uproar recently when she brought her toy poodle with her while attending a flea circus. The poodle stole _____.

Clue: What's the usual association between dogs and fleas?

10) What kind of degree do they give dogs that complete dog-training school? _____ degrees.
Clue: Play with the term used for college degrees.
Extra Clue: What do you call the sound a dog makes?

11) A man was locked in a room and told he couldn't come out until he made a pun. He immediately shouted, "_____ the door!" When he came out, he angrily quipped that anyone caught violently forcing others to create puns ought to be sentenced to do time in a _____.
Clue: What's the natural word to use here (first blank)?
Extra Clue: Use the word "pun" in each case.

12) Oliver Wendell Holmes once said that as a physician, he was grateful for small _____.
Clue: A play on a familiar phrase. What do you use thermometers for?

13) Two ropes walked into a fine restaurant. The waiter asked the first rope, "Are you one of them ropes?"
   "Why yes," stammered the rope.
   "Well, we don't serve your kind," said the waiter, as he threw him out.
   The second rope decided he'd better disguise himself, so he tied himself into a knot, and made his

two ends all ragged. The waiter then walked over and said, "How about you, are you one of them ropes?"

"I'm a _____," said the rope.

Clue: It's a way of saying "no," but of describing what he's just done to himself, as well.

Extra Clue: The key is the ragged ends of the rope.

14) Zsa Zsa Gabor (an actress from the 1950s) once remarked that, in spite of everyone's image of her, she really is a good housekeeper. In fact, every time she gets divorced, she _____.

Clue: Be literal about the quality in question.

15) A well-known singer was tired of singing alone all the time, but he could never get a partner to agree to join him. Finally, he solved the problem by going out and buying a(n) _____.

Clue: What do we generally buy when we don't want to pay someone else to do something? Use the term for two people singing together.

Extra Clue: It's a kind of kit.

16) We all pitied the poor cow that tried to jump over a barbed wire fence. It was a(n) _____ disaster.

Clue: A familiar phrase, which also refers to the part of the cow that milk comes from.

17) A friend of mine says he's tried every diet imaginable, but nothing has worked. Now he says, "I'm on a seafood diet. Every time I _____ food, I eat it."

Clue: None needed.

18) Doctor to teenage girl (putting his stethoscope to his ears): "Big breaths."

   Patient: "Yeth, and I'm not even _____."

Clue: The key is the word "yeth." She always talks this way.

19) When do doctors get most annoyed?

   When they're out of _____.

Clue: Whom do doctors treat?

20) What do you call a cow that's just delivered its offspring? _____.

Clue: Think of a kind of coffee. What kind do you drink if you're concerned about the harmful effects of coffee?

21) Did you hear about the (fill in the name of any group you want to put down) who took his wife to Domino's Pizza when she went into labor? He heard they had _____.

Clue: What service did Domino's Pizza pioneer?

22) What's the best Christmas gift for the person who has everything? _____.

Clue: Find another interpretation of "has everything." In this case, having everything is not good.

Extra Clue: He's ill.

23) Why wouldn't the skeleton cross the road?

   He didn't have the _____.

Clue: A familiar phrase meaning "didn't have the courage."

24) How can a pitcher win a baseball game without ever throwing a ball? By _____.
Clue: He really does throw a ball … and yet he doesn't.
Extra Clue: What does the umpire call it?

25) A father looked outside and saw his own children and their playmates pressing their hands into the cement of his newly laid sidewalk. He ran to the door and angrily gave the kids a real tongue-lashing. His shocked wife asked, "Don't you love your children?"
   He answered, "In the abstract, yes; but not in _____."
Clue: Another word for what sidewalks are made of.

26) A photographer went into a haunted castle, determined to get a photo of a ghost that was said to appear only once in a hundred years. Not wanting to frighten off the ghost, he waited in the dark until midnight, when the apparition appeared. The ghost turned out to be very friendly, and consented to pose for one photo. The happy photographer popped a bulb into his camera and took the picture. He discovered later in his studio that the photo was underexposed and completely blank. So the _____ was willing, but the _____ was weak.
Clue: A familiar phrase about yielding to temptation.

27) Cannibals captured a shipwrecked sailor. Each day, the natives would cut his arm with a dagger and drink some of his blood. Finally, he asked to see the king: "Look," he said, "if you're going to kill me and

eat me, go ahead, but I'm sick and tired of getting
_____ for the drinks."
Clue: The person who pays for everyone in a bar.
Extra Clue: What do you a call a car that's in the mud
and can't go?

28) A man said he'd recently bought a _____
house. "The real-estate broker told me one story
before I bought it and another story afterward."
Clue: A house with two floors.

29) (My favorite joke from my high school years.)
Three Native American women are sitting around a
fire. The first, sitting on a bearskin, has a son who
weighs 170 pounds. The second, sitting on a deerskin,
has a son who weighs 130 pounds. The third, sitting
on a hippopotamus hide, weighs 300 pounds. What
famous theorem does this illustrate?
   The _____ on the _____ is equal
to the _____ of the _____ on the other two
_____.
Clue: It's the Pythagorean Theorem.

30) A marine biologist recently discovered a way to
enable porpoises to live forever. But this unfortunately
required him to feed them a particular species of baby
sea gulls every day—and these gulls were on the
endangered species list. One night, while driving
home with a fresh load of baby gulls, he ran over a lion
that was reposing in the middle of the highway,
smoking a corncob pipe and reading a book.

A policeman witnessed this, and immediately
arrested him for transporting _____-____ gulls across
a _____ lion for _____ porpoises.
Clue: A multiple play on a familiar phrase. A driver
really can be arrested for the underlying idea
represented here. (This is admittedly corny, but fun.)

31) (This is not actually a joke, but the pun is still
there.) Statement by an announcer at the 2000
Olympics in Sydney: "Here come the athletes and their
_____."
Clue: Find another word for "fans." This word has an
extra meaning for male athletes.

32) (A children's riddle) What do the French give a
skeleton for Valentine's Day?
_____ in a heart-shaped box.
Clue: What's the generic French name for candy? So,
since this is a skeleton …

33) (Another children's riddle) Why do demons and
ghouls hang out together? Because _____ are a
_____ friend.
Clue: Sung by Marilyn Monroe in one of her movies.

34) Patient to eye doctor: "I'm very worried about the
outcome of this operation, doctor. What are my
chances?"
   Eye doctor to patient: "Don't worry, you won't be
able to _____ the difference."
Clue: The doctor's reassurance isn't very reassuring.

35) Madness takes its _____. Please have exact change.
Clue: On a turnpike, some lanes require exact change.

36) One guy says to another, "My wife's an angel!" The other guy says, "You're lucky, mine's _____."
Clue: Think of another way of interpreting "angel." The second guy is unhappy in his marriage.
Extra Clue: The assumption here is that you become an angel after you die.

37) A guy walks into a psychiatrist's office and says, "Doctor, you've got to help me! I keep thinking I'm a deck of cards!" The doctor says, "Sit over there. I'll _____ later."
Clue: When you're playing cards, what are you doing when you give each person their cards?

38) Leif Erikson, the famous Viking explorer, returned home from a long voyage and found his name missing from the town register. He complained to a local civic official, who apologized profusely, saying, "I must have taken _____ off my _____."
Clue: This is a familiar phrase which means "I must have lost my mind."

39) William Tell and his wife were known to be avid bowlers and even bowled in a league. But all the league records were destroyed in a fire, so we'll never know for whom the _____.
Clue: Think Hemingway book titles.

40) In the early 1800's the Tates Watch Company was know for their quality watches. They decided to extend their business to compasses for all the pioneers moving west. But their compasses were of poor quality. They were so bad that people often ended up in Canada or Mexico. This was the origin of the well-known expression, "He who _____ is lost."
Clue: The phrase means that you have to seize the opportunity when it arises.

41) People are very upset about the idea of cloning humans. But if they succeed at this, we'll all have to remember that clones are people _____.
Clue: Also. But find a way to make it funny using the idea of "also."

42) A skeptical anthropologist was cataloging South American folk remedies with the help of a tribal doctor who said that the leaves of a specific fern were a sure cure for constipation. When the tribal doctor saw the doubt in the anthropologist's face, he said, "Let me assure you, many of our local villagers have come to me and said, 'With _____ like these, who needs _____?'"
Clue: The familiar phrase refers to friends who turn out not to really be friends.

43) A man walks into a psychiatrist's office and shouts, "Doctor, doctor, I think I'm shrinking!" The doctor calmly says, "Now settle down. You'll just have to be a _____ patient."
Clue: If he really were shrinking, he would be shorter, right?

44) Santa's elves are nothing more than a bunch of
_____ clauses.
Clue: In English grammar, a part of a sentence.

45) Companies caught polluting the air should be
taken to court and charged with a _____-demeanor.
Clue: Water in the air. Less serious than a felony.

46) What kind of milk do you get from a pampered
cow? _____ milk.
Clue: It's not drinkable anymore. Some parents do
this to their children.

47) What do you call cheese that isn't yours?
_____ cheese.
Clue: An appetizer or something to eat with a beer.

48) What do prisoners use to telephone each other?
Clue: Where to prisoners sleep?

49) What kind of path do crazy people take through
the forest? A _____ path.
Clue: Hitchcock film.

50) How do you get Holy water? Boil the _____ out
of it.
Clue: Hot.

Answers to Puns

1) philately (flattery)
2) Jung (young)
3) dents (dance)
4) coverage
5) turtle (total)
6) ahead ("head" is sometimes used to refer to toilets or urinals)
7) retire
8) grounds
9) the show
10) Barkalaureate
11) O-pun ... punitentiary
12) fevers
13) frayed knot (afraid not)
14) keeps the house
15) duet-yourself kit
16) udder (utter)
17) see food
18) thixteen
19) patients (patience)
20) Decaffeinated
21) free delivery
22) Antibiotics (or a good doctor, etc.)
23) guts
24) throwing only strikes
25) the concrete
26) spirit ... flash (flesh)
27) stuck
28) two-story

29) squaw (square) ... hippopotamus (hypotenuse) ...
    sons (sum) ... squaws (squares) ... hides (sides)
30) under-age ... staid (state) ... immortal (immoral)
31) supporters
32) Bone-bones (bon-bons)
33) demons (diamonds) ghouls (girl's) best
34) see
35) toll
36) still alive
37) deal with you
38) Leif ... census (leave of my senses)
39) Tells bowled
40) has a Tates (hesitates)
41) two (too)
42) fronds (ferns will also work) ... enemas (friends
    ... enemies)
43) little
44) subordinate
45) mist (mis)
46) Spoiled
47) Nacho (not your)
48) Cell phones
49) psycho
50) hell (or devil)

Signs and
Bumper Stickers

1) In front of a church: "Searching for a new look? Come in for a free _____-lift."
Clue: What is a common cosmetic surgery that women often have done?
Extra Clue: The word you want rhymes with the answer to the previous clue.

2) Over the massive front doors of a cathedral: "The Gates of Heaven." Below this sign was a small cardboard sign which read, "Please use _____."
Clue: The big doors are locked. If it weren't for the first sign, this wouldn't be funny.

3) When down in the mouth, remember _____. He came out all right.
Clue: This involves a Biblical whale.

4) "Fight _____ decay. Read the (put here the name of your most trusted publication; e.g., *The New York Times*, *Christian Science Monitor*, *Bible*, etc.)."
Clue: Think "dentist" and the way groups you don't agree with seem to distort things.

5) Above washing machine in a Laundromat: "Please remove _____ when the light goes out."
Clue: The sign is appropriate to this context, but has an extra meaning.

6) In department store: "Toilet out of order: Use _____ below."
Clue: Go downstairs.

7) Outside a disco: "The most exclusive disco in town. _____ welcome."
Clue: This certainly weakens the credibility of their claim.

8) In front of a house: "Will the person who took my step ladder please return it. Please be assured that if you do, no further _____ will be taken."
Clue: He won't press charges.

9) On a dock: "Safety ladder. Climb at _____."
Clue: A common reminder to use caution. This doesn't make it sound very safe."

10) In a department store: "Bargain basement _____."
Clue: Think of where a bargain basement should be, and put it somewhere else.

11) On the side of a manure truck: "_____ Trucking."

Clue: Use a cruder word for manure. The owner has used only the two initials of his name for the name of the company.

12) On a garbage truck: "Satisfaction guaranteed or double your _____ back."
Clue: It rhymes with the familiar phrase for getting your money back.

13) "The seminar on time travel will be held _____."
Clue: It wouldn't be funny if were two weeks from now.

14) "If you believe in telekinesis, raise _____."
Clue: No clue needed.

15) "Manure, $5 pre-packed. $1 _____ yourself."
Clue: You pack it yourself.

16) Notice in field: "The farmer allows hikers to cross the field free, but the bull _____."
Clue: Attacks.

17) On computer store door: "Out for a quick _____."
Clue: Out to lunch. Find the right computer term.

18) Outside a hotel: "Now hiring. We need _____-experienced people."
Clue: It sounds like they want people with no experience, but they really want experience in this particular area of work.

Extra Clue: Use another word for "hotel."

19) On a butcher's window: "We are pleased to
_____ you."
Clue: They are happy to serve you. But what is their
product?

20) In front of Podiatrist's office: "Time _____ all
_____."
Clue: Find the familiar phrase and reverse it.
Emotional traumas generally get better with time.

21) In a taxidermist's window: "We really know our
_____."
Clue: They are experts at what?

22) At an optometrist's office: "If you don't _____
what you're looking for, you've come to the right
place."
Clue: The idea is "find," but what kind of office is
this?

23) Outside a radiator repair shop: "Best place in town
to take a _____."
Clue: What do you call it when water spills out of the
radiator?

24) On an electrician's truck: "Let us remove your
_____."
Clue: Underwear.

25) In a pharmacy: "We _____ with accuracy."

17

Clue: This one word says both that they do and do not fill their prescriptions accurately.
Extra Clue: It starts with a "d."

Answers to Signs and Bumper Stickers

1) faith (face)
2) other entrance (or back door, etc.)
3) Jonah
4) truth (tooth)
5) all your clothes
6) floor
7) Everyone is
8) steps
9) your own risk
10) upstairs
11) B.S.
12) trash (cash)
13) two weeks ago, yesterday, etc.
14) my hand
15) do it
16) charges
17) byte (bite)
18) Inn (in)
19) meat (meet)
20) wounds ... heels (vs. heals all wounds)
21) stuff
22) see
23) leak (as in urinate)
24) shorts
25) dispense

From the
Mouths of Children

An excellent way to strengthen your humor skills is to practice seeing the world from a child's point of view. Children often say or do things that, while not funny in their own mind, are very funny to adults. They often do not have the same understanding of words that you have, since you see them in a very different context. Be on the lookout for opportunities to exercise your sense of humor in all of your interactions with children. In the following examples, there will often be many different answers that can make it funny. Only one is provided here, but remember that the one you come up with may be even funnier than the one given.

1) As they were on their way to church, a Sunday School teacher asked her young children, "And why do we have to keep quiet during church?" Her 4-year-old daughter answered, "Because people are _____." *Clue*: It wouldn't be funny if she said "praying." What do people sometimes do in church that they don't want to be caught doing?

2) Little Bobby's next-door neighbor had a baby who had the misfortune of being born without ears. When they arrived home from the hospital, they invited

20

Bobby's family over to see their new baby. Bobby's parents were very concerned that he would make some kind of wise crack about the baby, so they had a good long talk with him before going over. Bobby's dad said, "Now son, that poor baby was born without any ears. I want you to be on your best behavior and not say one word about his ears, or I'm really going to spank you when we get back home." "I promise not to mention his ears at all," said Bobby.

At the neighbor's house, Bobby leaned over and touched the baby's hand. He looked at the baby's mother and said, "Oh, what a beautiful baby. The baby has perfect little hands and perfect little feet. And just look at his pretty little eyes ... Did the doctor say he could see good?" The mother said, "Why yes, the doctor said his vision was fine." Bobby said, "Well, it's a good thing, because he sure can't
_____."

Clue: Well, he didn't say the word "ears," but why would he ask about his vision?

3) A little boy was in his uncle's wedding. As he was coming down the aisle, he would take two steps, stop and turn to the crowd (alternating between the bride's and groom's side). While facing the crowd, he would put his hands up like claws and roar loudly. So it went, step, step ROAR, step, step, ROAR, all the way down the aisle. Of course, the crowd was in tears from laughing so hard by the time he got to the front. But the little boy was getting more and more distressed from all the laughing and was near tears when he got to the pulpit. When asked what he was doing, he said, "I was being the _____."

Paul E. McGhee

Clue: What is the traditional role of a young boy in a wedding? Play with the words for this role.

4) Sam was golfing with a friend and his 80-year-old father. Amazingly, the 80-year-old did better than the two middle-aged men, getting two birdies during the day. Back at Sam's house, they were all having a drink to celebrate their games. Sam hoisted his glass and said, "Here's to birdies." Sam's 5-year-old son held up his glass of milk and said, "Here's to _____."
Clue: What do small children play with in their bathtub?

5) Noah's wife was called _____.
Clue: What famous woman in history is associated with the word "arc?"

6) According to the *Bible*, Christians should only have one wife or husband. This is called _____.
Clue: Some say this can happen in a marriage after 10 or 15 years.

7) A sweet little boy surprised his grandmother one morning by bringing her a cup of coffee. He made it himself and was so proud. As she took her first sip, he anxiously waited to hear how good it was. In fact, the grandmother had never had such bad coffee in her life, but wanted to drink it to show her appreciation. As she forced down the last few sips, she noticed three of those little green army guys in the bottom of the cup. She asked, "Honey, why are these army guys in the bottom of my cup?" Her grandson said, "You know

gramma, it's like on TV, 'The best part of waking up is
_____ in your cup.'"
Clue: If you know the commercial, this should be
easy.

8) Solomon, one of David's sons, had 300 wives and
700 _____.
Clue: The real word was "concubines." There are
several ways to play with the sound of this word.

9) Teacher: Didn't you promise to behave?
   Student: Yes ma'am.
   Teacher: And didn't I promise to punish you if you
didn't?
   Student: Yes ma'am. But since I _____,
I don't _____.
Clue: He's suggesting that an odd sense of fairness be
applied here.

10) Teacher: I hope I don't see you looking at Mary's
paper.
   Tommie: I _____.
Clue: It's a "smart aleck" answer. He plans to look at
Mary's paper.

11) Teacher: If you had 17 dollars and you asked your
father for two more, how many dollars would you
have?
   Student: Seventeen.
   Teacher: You don't know your arithmetic very well.
   Student: You _____.
Clue: You should get this without a clue.

12) A little girl asked her mother, "Can I go outside and play with the boys?" Her mother replied, "No, you can't play with the boys, they're too rough." The girl thought about it for a few seconds and asked, "If I can find a _____ one, can I play with him?"
Clue: "Rough" is the key word.

13) The Jews are a proud people, but throughout history they've had trouble with unsympathetic

_____.
Clue: It's a sexual word. What are non-Jews called?

14) A three-year-old put his shoes on by himself. His mother noticed that the left shoe was on the right foot. She said, "Son, your shoes are on the wrong feet." He raised his eyebrows and looked at her and said, "Oh no they're not, Mom. I know they're _____."
Clue: Find another way to interpret "wrong."

15) After the church service, a little boy told the pastor, "When I grow up, I'm going to give you some money."

    "Well thank you," the pastor replied, "but why?"

    "Because my daddy said you're one of the _____ preachers we've ever had."
Clue: His father said he wasn't a very good preacher.

16) A daddy was listening to his daughter say her prayers, and heard "Dear Harold." He stopped her, saying, "Wait a minute, why did you call God 'Harold'?" She said, "Well that's what they call him in church when we say that prayer, 'Our father

_____.'"

Clue: This is a familiar prayer, containing a word in the first line that she's sure to misunderstand.

17) A mother was preparing pancakes for her sons, Howard, 5, and Paul, 3. The boys started arguing over who would get the first pancake. The mother decided to use the moment for a moral lesson. She said, "If Jesus were sitting here, he would say, 'Let my brother have the first pancake. I can wait.'" Howard turned to his younger brother and said, "Paul, you _____."
Clue: Howard didn't learn the lesson. He still wanted to eat first.
Extra Clue: What do kids say when playing pretend games?

18) A kindergarten class was taking a field trip to a zoo. The teacher said they would see a 10-foot snake. One girl seemed puzzled by this, and the teacher asked what was wrong and if she was afraid of the snake. The girl said, "No, I just never saw a snake _____ before."
Clue: She didn't understand that the teacher was talking about the size of the snake.

19) A 4-year-old boy still had the habit if sucking his thumb, even though his mother had tried everything from bribery to reasoning to painting it with lemon juice to stop the habit. She finally resorted to threats, warning him that, "If you don't stop sucking your thumb, your stomach is going to blow up like a balloon."

Later that day, walking in the park, mother and son saw a pregnant woman sitting on a bench. The 4-year-old studied her seriously for a minute, and then said to her, "Uh-oh … I _____."

Clue: There are lots of ways to say it, but there could only be one thing that he's thinking.

20) Joshua led the Hebrews in the Battle of
_____.

Clue: A product that many older people drink.

21) A four-year-old boy went with his dad to see a new litter of kittens. When they got back home, the excited boy said to his mother, "There were two boy kittens and two girl kittens." "How did you know?" his mother asked. "Daddy picked them and looked underneath. I think it's _____ their bottom.

Clue: This boy is just learning to read.

22) Marie explained to her kindergarten teacher that she was very concerned about her grandmother because her veins were not far enough from each other. When the teacher asked what she meant, Marie clarified, saying, "Mommy said that she had
_____ veins."

Clue: What is a common problem with veins—especially as you get older?

23) Timmy: Teacher, would you punish me for something I didn't do?

   Teacher: Of course not.

   Timmy: Good, because I didn't
_____.

Clue: Timmy is manipulating and tricking the teacher.

24) The Seventh Commandment is "Thou shalt not
_____ adultery."   -
Clue: Even when people do commit adultery, what do
they generally not want to do afterwards?

25) Teacher: Sandra, make up a sentence that starts
with the letter "I."
   Sandra: I is …
   Teacher: No, no, Sandra, you must always say "I
am."
   Sandra: I am the _____.
Clue: What is the one kind of statement for which the
teacher would be wrong?

26) On the first day of school, the kindergarten
teacher said, "If anyone has to go to the bathroom,
hold up two fingers." A little voice from the back of
the room asked, "How will _____?"
Clue: Did the teacher really explain that this was to
request permission to go?

27) A mother and her young son returned from the
grocery store and began putting groceries away. He
opened a box of animal crackers and spread them out
on the table. "What are you doing?" his mother asked.
"The box says you can't eat them if the seal is broken.
I'm _____."
Clue: He misunderstood a key word on the box.

28) One day while watching her mother iron, a little
girl notices several white hairs that she never saw
before on her mother's head. Puzzled, she asks,
"Mom, why are some of your hairs white?" Her

mother replied, "Well, every time you do something wrong and make me cry or unhappy, one of my hairs turns white." The girl thought about it a minute and said, "Wow, you must have been pretty _____ when you were _____, all of _____."
Clue: She thought about her grandmother.

29) A father was at the beach with his children when his four-year-old son ran up to him, grabbed his hand, and led him to the shore, where a sea gull lay dead in the sand. "Daddy, what happened to him?" the son asked. "He died and went to Heaven," his dad answered. The boy thought a minute, and then said, "Did God _____?"
Clue: What do we sometimes do with things we don't want?

30) A teacher was giving a lesson about blood circulation. Trying to make it clearer, he said, "If I stood on my head, the blood would run into it, and I would turn red in the face." "Yes sir," said one of the boys, "but then why don't my feet turn red when I'm standing up in the usual position?" Another boy grinned and said, "Because your feet ain't _____."
Clue: It's ambiguous as to whether he's referring to the teacher or the first boy, but he's suggesting someone doesn't have too much upstairs.

31) For weeks, a six-year-old boy kept telling his first-grade teacher about the baby brother or sister that was expected at his house. One day, his mother allowed him to feel the movements of the unborn child. The boy was obviously impressed, but made no comment.

But he stopped telling his teacher about the impending event. One day the teacher finally asked him what had become of the baby brother or sister expected at his house. The boy burst into tears and confessed, "I think Mommy _____!"
Clue: What might a young child think about feeling the baby's movements in his mother's stomach?

32) A father was reading Bible stories to his young son. He read, "A man named Lot was warned to take his wife and flee from the city and not look back. But his wife looked back and was turned to salt."

His son asked, "What happened to _____?"
Clue: Assume that he didn't understand the word "flee."

33) A nine-year-old was asked to name the 10 Commandments in any order. His answer was

_____ _____.
Clue: Nine-year-olds can be pretty literal.

34) An eighth-grade class was discussing the qualifications for being President of the United States. When the teacher explained that you must be a natural-born citizen, a girl raised her hand and asked, "Does that mean if you were born _____, you can't be President?"
Clue: She misunderstood "natural-born."
Extra Clue: Think of the birth process itself.

35) An honest seven-year-old calmly explained to her parents that an older boy had kissed her after class. Her mother gasped, "How did that happen?" "Well, it

29

wasn't easy," added the girl, "three girls
_____."
Clue: It's just the opposite of what you think.

36) A boy was overheard telling another child
following his Sunday School class that Solomon was
very wise, and that he had many wives and also many

_____.

Clue: He was confused about the word "concubines."

37) A three-year-old was watching her mother breast-
feed the new baby. After a while, she pointed to the
mother's breast and asked, "What's that?"
   "That's where the baby gets its milk," her mother
explained. After a while, the baby was moved to the
other side to continue feeding. The three-year-old
asked, "So what's that, _____?"
Clue: There are two main liquids the three-year-old
drinks, so maybe the same is true for the baby.

38) A boy taking a high school chemistry class wrote
on an exam that water is composed of two kinds of
_____, hydrogen and oxygen.
Clue: Eli Whitney.
Extra Clue: Cotton.

39) A woman gets on a bus with her young daughter.
The rules are that children ride free until age five. The
girl just walks by the driver, who says, "Just a minute
little girl, how old are you?" "Four and a half." "And
when will you be five?" "As soon as I
_____."
Clue: The girl is honest. She's really five now.

40) A five-year-old boy is in a drug store. He picks up a box of Tampax and takes it to the counter to pay for it. The cashier says, "Are you sure this is what you want?" The boy nods and says, "Yes, I'm sure. It says right here on the box that with these, you can

_____, _____, and _____, and I can't _____."

Clue: This is very difficult. Think of some things a five-year-old can't do, but would like to be able to do.

Paul E. McGhee

Answers to From the Mouths of Children

1) sleeping
2) wear glasses
3) ring bear (bearer)
4) duckies
5) Joan of Arc
6) monotony (monogamy)
7) soldiers (Folgers)
8) porcupines
9) didn't keep my promise … expect you to keep yours
10) hope you don't either
11) don't know my father
12) smooth
13) genitals (gentiles)
14) my feet
15) poorest
16) who art in Heaven, hallowed (Harold) be Thy name
17) be Jesus
18) with any feet
19) know what you've been doing
20) Geritol (Jericho)
21) printed on
22) very close (varicose)
23) do my homework
24) admit (commit)
25) ninth letter of the alphabet

26) that help
27) looking for the seal
28) bad … little … grandma's hairs are white
29) throw him back down? (Other answers also work.)
30) empty
31) ate it
32) the flea (flee)
33) 3, 6, 2, 9, 7, etc.
34) Cesarean
35) helped me catch him
36) porcupines
37) juice (or water)
38) gin
39) get off this bus
40) swim, play tennis … ride a bicycle … do any of those things

Printed Mistakes

Mistakes are commonly made in church bulletins, notes from parents to teachers and other communications. These mistakes are often funny and provide an additional opportunity for you to practice spotting opportunities for verbal humor.

Parent Notes

1) Please excuse David for being absent yesterday. He was sick and I had him _____.
Clue: He got a vaccination.

2) Please excuse Sally for being absent. She had _____ and her boots leak.
Clue: This will make no sense, even after you get it. These are two conditions which have nothing to do with each other, but are funny when put together.

3) My son is under a doctor's care and should not take P.E. today. Please _____ him.
Clue: She meant to say "excuse."

4) Please excuse Robert for being absent yesterday. He had a cold and could not _____ well.
Clue: The intended word was "breathe."

5) Please excuse John's absence from school yesterday. He had very loose _____.
Clue: It rhymes with bowels.

6) Please excuse Gloria from Jim today. She is

_____.
Clue She meant menstruating (which makes it funnier, since she misspelled "gym").

7) Please excuse Diane for being absent yesterday. She was in bed with _____.
Clue: She meant cramps.

Church Bulletins

8) The topic for this evening's sermon will be "What is Hell?" Come early and listen to our

_____.
Clue: This is a coincidental pairing of ideas. Think music.

9) Next Sunday is Easter Sunday. The crafts teacher, Mrs. Thompson, will come up and ____ an egg on the altar.
Clue: She's going to put one there. Find a word that communicates this with a double meaning.

10) For all of you who have _____ and don't know it, we have a nursery downstairs.
Clue: Why would you need a nursery?

11) If worry and anxiety are killing you, let the church

_____.

Clue: This makes it sound like the church will finish off the process of killing you with worry.

12) A bean supper will be held on Thursday evening in the church hall. _____ will follow.
Clue: It's not prayer. It's a special interpretation of an unfortunate side effect of eating beans.

13) The Ladies' Liturgy Society will meet Tuesday evening. Mrs. Wilson will sing "Put me in my little bed," _____ by the pastor.
Clue: The pastor will sing too, but this word makes it sound inappropriate.

14) The rosebud on the altar this morning is to announce the birth of James Ronald Towson, the _____ of Reverend and Mrs. Towson.
Clue: It's a boy. What one letter could you change in the word (analogous to "daughter") and make it funny in the context of the church's pastor?

15) Please remember in your prayers the many who are sick ____ our church and community.
Clue: Choosing the wrong two-letter word here completely changes the meaning.

16) A meeting of the Little Mothers Club will be held Tuesday at 5 p.m. All wishing to _____ little mothers, please see the minister in his study.
Clue: There is an inappropriate sexual allusion here.

17) Weight Watchers will meet at 7 p.m. Please use the _____ at the side entrance.

Clue: What kind of door would make this funny, given the nature of the group?

18) The choir invites any member of the congregation who enjoys _____ to join the choir.
Clue: Again, play with the word that describes what a choir does. There is a mistake in one letter.

19) Item listed in bulletin announcements during the minister's illness: God is good. Reverend McAlister is _____.
Clue: This makes the minister sound pretty impressive. He's not as sick as he was.

20) The third verse of Blessed Assurance will be sung without musical _____.
Clue: It will be sung acapella. This is not a pun. The mistake suggests that the singing will not be very good.

21) Ushers will _____ latecomers.
Clue: There's a letter missing here.

22) The audience is asked to remain seated until the end of the _____.
Clue: The real word is what you play at the end of a church service. This mistake is an economic trend.

23) The Bible study class will meet at 6 p.m. Wednesday evening. Refreshments will be served after the _____.
Clue: This is an innocent abbreviation that takes on a crude meaning here.

24) The Visitation committee is requesting 10 additional volunteers to make calls on people not _____ with any church.
Clue: The intended word means "associated" and begins with "a." The mistaken word also begins with "a." The mistake that makes it funny here has three syllables.

25) The low self-esteem group will meet Tuesday from 7 to 8:30 p.m. Please use the _____ door.
Clue: What door is consistent with low self-esteem?

Answers to Printed Mistakes

Parent Notes

1) shot
2) diarrhea
3) execute
4) breed
5) vowels
6) administrating
7) gramps

Church Bulletins

8) choir practice
9) lay
10) infants
11) help
12) music
13) accompanied
14) sin (son)
15) of (should be "in")
16) become
17) large double doors (or any other large door)
18) sinning (singing)
19) better
20) accomplishment (vs. accompaniment)
21) eat (seat)
22) recession (recessional)
23) B.S. (Bible study)
24) afflicted (affiliated)
25) back

Headlines

Your newspaper probably uses play on words to create headlines. Use these examples to practice, but start today looking for wordplay in headlines on your own.

1) Energizer Bunny arrested, charged with _____.
Clue: Assault.

2) _____ opposition expected to new cemetery proposal.
Clue: A slang term for a dead person.

3) Hospitals sued by _____ foot doctors.
Clue: How many?

4) _____ week starts with a bang.
Clue: It's sexual.
Extra Clue: You use these to prevent pregnancy.

5) Iraqi head seeks _____.
Clue: Guns.

6) Juvenile court to try _____ defendant.
Clue: He shot someone.
Extra Clue: Add "ing."

7) Teacher _____ idle kids.

Clue: The teachers are refusing to work. Make it plural.

8) New obesity study looks for _____ test group.
Clue: They need a bigger sample size.

9) Kids _____ nutritious snacks.
Clue: They're creating their own snacks.

10) Drunk gets six months in _____case.
Clue: Think musical instruments.

11) _____ tires out.
Clue: A kind of tire often used in snow and ice.
Extra Clue: This tire damages the road.

12) Lung cancer in women _____.
Clue: Increases. Think fungus (a fungus we eat).

13) Thief caught stealing clock; faces _____.
Clue: He'll go to prison.

14) Man without ears waives court _____.
Clue: Appearance.

15) Local school dropouts _____.
Clue: Reduced by 50%. But make it sound deadly.

16) Arson suspect _____ in Detroit fire.
Clue: He was arrested and is being kept in jail. But this makes it sound like he's being burned in the fire.

17) Stolen Renoir found by _____.

Clue: Any inanimate object.

18) Trees can _____ wind.
Clue: Stop or reduce.

19) Publicize your business absolutely free. Send _____ for details.
Clue: Well, then it's not really free, is it?

20) "Would I climb to the top of ____ Everest again? Absolutely!"
Clue: This is a mistake. "Mt." was intended.

Answers to Headlines

1) battery   2) Stiff
3) seven (or any other number)
4) Condom   5) arms
6) shooting   7) strikes
8) larger   9) make
10) violin (or any other musical instrument, or anything that is associated with a case)
11) Stud   12) mushrooms
13) time   14) hearing
15) cut in half.   16) held
17) tree (toilet, desk, etc.).   18) break
19) $10 (or any other amount).
20) Mr.

Oxymorons

No clues are given in this section. By definition, an oxymoron involves two words or ideas that are intrinsically incompatible with one another. Just look for a familiar phrase that includes this opposition. Remember that in some cases more than one word will work here. The key is the general category of word used.

1) Could you give me an exact _____ of the cost?
2) He went to Rio on a working _____.
3) That's a _____ ugly dog.
4) Just try to act _____.
5) The money was found _____ Saturday night.
6) We use efficient synthetic _____ gas.
7) I was _____ pleased by the workmanship on the project.
8) He _____ misunderstood what I said.
9) He's learning _____ basic computer language.
10) A Peanuts character often said, "_____ grief."
11) He's always almost _____ on time.
12) Please leave. We'd like to be alone _____.
13) I really like _____ rock music.
14) Parting is such sweet _____.
15) Now, _____, let's have a look at that sore knee.
16) He likes to wear tight _____.
Clue: A name for pants.

17) Giving gifts at Thanksgiving is a new _____.
18) I just received an important message via wireless _____.
19) I'd like a nondairy _____ for my coffee.
20) I refuse to put wine in this _____ glass.
21) Please give me an original _____ of the letter.
22) Take the elevated _____ train.
23) The touchdown came on a _____ lateral.
24) The Great Salt Lake is rapidly becoming a ____ lake.
25) The restaurant only serves _____ shrimp. (This is the classic oxymoron.)

Answers to Oxymorons

1) estimate	2) vacation
3) pretty	4) natural
5) missing	6) natural
7) terribly	8) clearly
9) advanced	10) Good
11) exactly	12) together
13) soft	14) sorrow
15) then	16) slacks
17) tradition	18) cable
19) creamer	20) plastic
21) copy	22) subway
23) forward	24) dry
25) jumbo/giant	

Jokes

.

1) Q: Why are lawyers buried 20 feet deep?
   A: Because _____ they're good people.
Clue: A familiar phrase meaning, "in their heart."

2) Lawyer to client: "Have you ever been up before this judge?"
   Client: "Well, I don't know, what
   _____?"
Clue: Find another meaning of "been up before."

3) A woman wrote to a newspaper columnist, expressing concern about her 30-year-old daughter and her roommate who didn't seem to want to have anything to do with men. She asked, "Do you think they could be _____?"
Clue: She's confused about the term "lesbian."
Extra Clue: The term refers to a specific nationality.

4) "Say, I heard Mrs. Cargle in Room 324 had triplets."
   "Yes … they say it happens once in 10,000 times."
   "Amazing! How does she find time to
   _____?"
Clue: There is confusion about the meaning of "10,000 times."
Extra Clue: She is applying "10,000 times" to Mrs. Cargle alone.

5) What's the most frequently heard phrase at the surgeon's annual ball? "May I _____?"
Clue: What do you say when you want to dance with someone else's dance partner?

6) A doctor made a terrible mistake, and left a sponge inside the patient after surgery. There were no side effects, except that the patient was always _____.
Clue: What is the main property of a sponge?

7) What did the doctor say to the patient after removing his appendix? "That'll be enough _____."
Clue: This is something you might say to a kid who makes a "wise crack."

8) "I'm getting to the age that my mind's starting to wander. But I guess I shouldn't worry, it can't _____."
Clue: This is a put-down of oneself. If you weren't too bright, how would this influence the meaning of "wander?"

9) What is the oldest known form of oral contraception?
Clue: Think about the ambiguity of the word "oral."

10) What do you call investors who wait around to buy up bankrupt firms? _____ capitalists.
Clue: Come up with a variation of "venture capitalists." Change the word "venture."

11) What's the difference between a teacher and a railroad conductor? One _____ the _____ and the other _____ the _____.
Clue: Use the words "train" and "mind."

12) They let commercial pilots start flying these days with almost no experience. Last week, the pilot of the plane I flew in was so new at the job that the plane had _____.
Clue: How do kids learn to ride a bicycle?

13) (As a roast) In his long career, he has consistently done the work of two men, _____ and _____.
Clue: Name and two people who are known to be incompetent bunglers.

14) A nurse just out of nursing school hadn't yet learned that the polite word for "bedpan" in this hospital was "vase." She was about to leave a male patient's room when he asked, "Nurse, would you bring me a vase right away?"
    "Sure, Mister Talbert," she said, "How big is your _____?"
Clue: A natural error, if you don't know the hospital meaning of "vase." (But note the ambiguous meaning you're left with in this joke.)

15) During a period of heavy flooding in town, everyone was asked to get shots to prevent an outbreak of typhoid. The place residents had to go for their shots depended on where they lived. One woman,

after showing her identification to the staff was told, "Lady, you'll have to get your shot in your precinct."

"How come?" she asked. "All the others are getting their shots in their _____."
Clue: She misunderstands "precinct."

16) When the doctor answered the phone, a frantic father was shouting, "Come quick, Doc, my little boy swallowed a condom!"

The doctor hung up, grabbed his bag, and was running out the door when the phone rang again. "Never mind, Doc," said the boy's father, "I found _____."
Clue: The concern was not for the boy's well being. Assume that the only concern here was sexual.

17) "Call me a cab!"
   "OK, _____."
Clue: Look for a second meaning of a key word.

18) A man got his wife a toy poodle for her birthday. But she almost killed it trying to get the _____ into it.
Clue: What's often missing from toys kids get for Christmas?

19) There was this guy whose conscience was bothering him because he cheated on his income tax. So he wrote a letter to IRS, and said, "Dear sir: Five years ago, I cheated on my income tax. I haven't been able to sleep a wink since. Enclosed, please find $500. If I still can't sleep, I'll _____."

Clue: A remark that draws attention to something he really doesn't want to draw attention to.

20) "Doctor, my husband thinks he's a chicken."
  "How long has this been going on?"
  "About five years."
  "Well why haven't you brought him in sooner?"
  "Well, to tell you the truth, up 'til now we needed
  _____."
Clue: The husband is not the only one who has the delusion.

21) Obstetricians' motto: "Always at your
  _____."
Clue: Wordplay on a part of the anatomy.

22) A doctor calls in a very anxious patient and says, "I'm afraid I have bad news and worse news. The bad news is that your tests were positive, and you have 24 hours to live."
  "Good Lord!" said the patient, "What could be worse?"
  "The worse news," said the doctor, "is that I got the results _____ and _____."
Clue: What would lead the patient to have even less than 24 hours?

23) What does "paradox" mean? _____.
Clue: Make three words out of this word.

24) The gynecologist looked up after completing his examination. "I'm sorry, miss, but removing that

vibrator is going to involve a lengthy and delicate operation."

"I'm not sure I can afford it," sighed the woman. "Why don't you just replace _____?"
Clue: If it's too expensive to remove, she may as well get some use out of it while it's there.

25) A man is in the hospital to have his gangrene-infected leg amputated. He wakes up after the operation and asks, "How'm I doin' doc?"

"Well, I've got some good news, and some bad news. The bad news is that we amputated the wrong leg."

"My god! I can't believe it," says the patient. "What's the good news?"

"Your other leg _____."
Clue: No clue necessary.

26) Think of another way to say, "The sausage has not yet arrived."

"The _____ is yet to _____."
Clue: Start with a German word that means sausage. It's a phrase you've heard before.

27) Did you hear about the two angels who got kicked out of heaven? They were trying to _____ a

_____.
Clue: This is a double pun. It's sexual.
Extra Clue: Find a phrase that means to make money.

28) Item on news broadcast. "The Detroit Police Department reported today that someone broke into Police Headquarters during the night and damaged

their toilet facilities. The sabotage remains a mystery, and at present the police have nothing to _____."
Clue: No clue necessary.

29) Why did the elephants quit their job at the factory?
They got tired of working for _____.
Clue: They were underpaid.

30) Did you hear about the tomcat that ate cheese so he could look down rat holes with _____ breath?
Clue: What do we use minnows for when fishing?

31) An Iowa farmer visits his cousin in New York. They come out of a restaurant and find it raining. "Oh no," said the farmer, "It's raining cats and dogs. It's the worst thing that could happen during my visit."
    "Oh, there's something worse than that," said the New Yorker, "_____ taxis."
Clue: Calling taxis. A familiar bad-weather event.

32) What do you call a clairvoyant midget running from the law?
    A(n) _____ at _____.
Clue: Use the names of the three traditional clothing sizes.

33) "I have a delicious piece of gossip to tell you, but listen carefully. I can only tell it once, because I promised that I wouldn't _____."
Clue: The understanding was to not tell anyone, but technically the person can tell it once, because the agreement was to not _____.

34) A harried resident was walking down the hospital corridor when a nurse stopped him. "Dr. Thomas," she whispered, "you've got a thermometer stuck behind your ear."

"Hell!" he yelled. "Some _____ has my pen."

Clue: Where are thermometers sometimes placed?

35) An elderly woman, assumed to be unconscious, is wheeled into the emergency room. The paramedic says, "She's critical." The woman opens her eyes and says, "_____! _____."

Clue: How might she react to the "other" meaning of "critical?"

36) How many Yuppies does it take to change a light bulb?

Two. One to mix the _____ and one to call the _____.

Clue: Would a Yuppie do it him/herself?

37) Why are surgeons funnier than other doctors?
Because they keep their patients _____.

Clue: Another way of saying they keep their patients laughing.

38) A German had to have surgery while visiting the U.S. The doctor asked if he wanted a local anesthetic. He said, "Well, I'd really prefer a _____ one."

Clue: The key word is "local." Remember, the patient comes from another country.

39) A patient asked the doctor why his lower back was always stiff as a board. "Well, that's not surprising," said the doctor, "that's the _____ region of your back."
Clue: What the name of the place you go to get two-by-fours and other large pieces of wood?

40) An unfortunate five-year-old girl got very sick after swallowing a nickel, two dimes, and three pennies. The doctors treated her for weeks, but there was _____.
Clue: She didn't improve.

41) "Our next speaker is tall, dark, and handsome. Wait, I misread that. He's tall and, in the _____, handsome."
Clue: No clue needed here.

42) "I'd like to introduce the entire panel to you. From right to left, and this is not a _____ ..."
Clue: Find another way to interpret "right to left."

43) I know a clothing salesman who has a hundred suits, and they're all _____.
Clue: Look for a legal meaning of the word "suit."

44) "Order! Order in the court!"
"_____ please, your Honor."
Clue: Look for a simple pun here.

45) A man asked a lawyer what his fee was.
   "Fifty dollars for three questions," said the lawyer.

"That's pretty steep, isn't it?"

"Yes. Now what's your _____?"

Clue: He's a lawyer, so you'd better take him literally.

46) There's a gate separating heaven and hell. One day it gets knocked down, and St. Peter goes to examine the damage. He calls the devil and says, "The gate's down again. It's your turn to fix it."

"Forget it," says the devil, "my people are much too busy."

"But we had a deal," says St. Peter, "and if you don't honor it, we'll sue you for breach of contract."

"Right," says the devil, "and just where are you going to find a _____ up here?"

Clue: No clue needed.

47) Two mice are chatting in a laboratory: "And how are you getting along with your professor?"

"Oh, great! Every time I _____, he _____."

Clue: Think about Pavlov and his conditioned dogs.

48) A man runs into the ER and yells, "My wife's having a baby in the cab!" So the doctor grabs his stuff, rushes out to the cab, lifts the lady's dress, and begins to take off her underwear. Suddenly, he notices that there are _____, and he's in _____.

Clue: It's a big hospital. What's the biggest blunder a doctor could make in this situation?

49) He's not much of a musician. He doesn't even know the difference between _____ and Acapulco.

Clue: A way of singing.

50) Where do you get dragon milk?
   From cows with _____.
Clue: Play with the sound of "dragon."

51) What do you get if you cross a dog and a chicken?
   _____ eggs.
Clue: Combine a familiar word for "dog" with a way of preparing eggs to eat.

52) What do you get when you cross an owl and a pig?
   A bird that gives you _____.
Clue: An owl seems to stare at you. Pigs like to wallow in dirt and mud.

53) Anna's mother has three daughters. The youngest is named Penny. The middle one is named Nickel. What is the name of the oldest daughter?
Clue: It's a tricky question, but not a trick. All the information you need is present in the question.

54) What to you get when you cross a bale of straw with an octopus? A _____ with _____ handles.
Clue: A strange sweeping device.

55) What do you get when you cross a parrot with a hyena? An animal that can _____ what it's _____.
Clue: What is each species known for?

56) What do you get when you cross a woodpecker with a carrier pigeon? A bird that
_____ when it _____.
Clue: How do you know when a carrier pigeon arrives?

57) What do you get when you cross a robin and a ballpoint pen? A bird with a(n) _____.
Clue: What is an important feature of most ballpoint pens (a feature you use when you're through writing)?

58) What do you get when you cross a hippopotamus with a peanut butter sandwich?
A _____ that _____ to the _____.
Clue: What happens to your mouth when you eat a peanut butter sandwich?

59) What do you get when you cross an elephant with the family dog? A very _____.
Clue: This is not a typical cross joke. Think about the stereotypic relationship between mailmen and dogs.

60) How are a duck and an icicle alike? They both grow _____.
Clue: Think of ski jackets known for their warmth.

61) "It's raining cats and dogs outside."
   "I know, I just stepped in a _____."
Clue: Take what's left on the ground after it rains, and change the sound so that it becomes the name of a small indoor dog.

62) A man walks into a bar in a tough neighborhood and asks, "What do you have on ice?" The bartender says, "You wouldn't know _____."
Clue: What else might be put on ice or in another cool place in a tough neighborhood? (Actually, this is generally done in a morgue.)

63) What's the difference between an elephant and a jar of peanut butter? The elephant doesn't

_____.
Clue: You've already seen a variation of this.

64) Q: What's today's weather forecast for Baghdad? (A joke circulating during the first war with Iraq.)
  A: Cloudy and windy, with temperatures in the

_____.
CLUE: There were rumors of the possibility of dropping a "limited" nuclear bomb on Baghdad.

65) Q: What do Hiroshima, Nagasaki, and Baghdad have in common? (Another joke circulating during the war with Iraq.)
  A: _____.
Clue: Yes, it has something to do with nuclear bombs, but find some way of adding an unexpected twist to the answer.

66) My husband's really not too bright. He went to the Burgher King last week, and someone stole the car while he was inside. I asked him, "Did you see what the guy looked like?"
  He said, "No but I got _____."

Clue: An observation that's generally helpful—except when it's your own car.

67) A tailor was robbed, and the police asked if he could describe the guy. He said, "Of course I can, he was a _____."
Clue: What terms do tailors use on their jobs?

68) "I just saw a man-eating shark in the aquarium!"
   "Big deal! I just saw a man eating _____ in the restaurant."
Clue: Look for a second interpretation of "man-eating shark."

69) My mother just got a new job. She's a travel agent for guilt _____.
Clue: Something stereotypically associated with certain mothers.

70) After years of research, scientists have finally concluded that the fetus becomes viable after
_____ _____.
Clue: You should be able to come up with an answer to this. Exaggerate! A second answer provided here is impossible to guess, but will be appreciated by parents with adult children living at home.

71) A father tells his teenage daughter, "There are two words I'd like you to drop from your vocabulary. One is 'awesome,' and the other is 'gross'."
   "OK," she said, "What _____?"

Clue: Think of a second way of interpreting what the father is saying. The daughter doesn't realize that he's talking about dropping these two specific words.

72) Why did the cookie cry?
   Because it's mother had been a _____ so long.
Clue: It's a kind of cookie. This is a children's joke.

73) My daughter thinks I'm too nosy. At least that's what she scribbled in her _____.
Clue: The one place that shows that the daughter is right.

74) In my teens, my mother always said, "The way you put things off, you'll never amount to anything."
   I said, "Oh yeah, just _____."
Clue: Technically, this shows his mother was right.

75) As two politicians discuss strategies, the Democrat says, "Whenever I take a cab, I give the driver a large tip and say, 'Vote Democratic'."
   The Republican says, "I have a similar approach. Whenever I take a cab, I _____, and say, 'Vote Democratic'."
Clue: Remember, this is a Republican talking, so if he says the same thing as the Democrat, is he really doing the same thing with the cab driver?

76) The controversy about giving aid to the Contras in Nicaragua in the 1980s has finally been resolved. When President Reagan made a favorable statement about "contraceptives," Ollie North misunderstood him, thinking he said "_____."

Clue: Turn the word "contraceptives" around.

77) Did you hear about George W. Bush's new fast-food chicken franchise in Texas? They only serve _____ wings.
Clue: What are the classic labels for conservative and liberal politics?

78) What would it take to legalize marijuana these days?

A _____ session of congress.
Clue: You probably don't need a clue for this.

79) A father picked up his son Daren from school one day. Knowing that the final selection of parts for a big school play were being posted that day, he asked if he got a part. Daren enthusiastically answered, "Yes, I play a man who's been married for 20 years."

"That's great, son. Keep up the good work and before you know it they'll be giving you a _____ part."
Clue: Refers to a stereotypic view of one aspect of marital relationships.

80) How can you tell when a politician is lying?

His lips _____.
Clue: A stereotypic view of politicians.

81) They're finally getting around to putting a clock on the Leaning Tower of Pisa. Now they'll have both the time and the _____.
Clue: Plays on a familiar phrase, in which one has the time to do something, but does not want to do it.

82) Two women walk into a club for men only. The waiter comes over and says, "I'm sorry ladies, but we only serve men here."

One of the women answers, "Oh good, _____."
Clue: The key word is serve.

83) Two lawyers (put your favorite victim here) were out walking in the woods when they came upon a set of tracks. One lawyer said, "Those are wolf tracks." The other said, "No, they're bear tracks." Just then, they both looked up and got hit by a _____.
Clue: They were both wrong. They were hit by something moving fast.

84) A man tells his psychiatrist, "It was terrible. I was in Europe on business, and I wired my wife that I'd be back a day early. I rushed home from the airport and found her in bed with my best friend. How could she do this to me?"

The psychiatrist pauses reflectively and says, "Well, maybe she _____."
Clue: The psychiatrist is not giving the support the client expects. But his answer does make sense in another way.

85) How many psychiatrists does it take to screw in a light bulb?

Only one, but the bulb must really _____.
Clue: Psychiatrists help people change their behavior. But what is usually the first step?

86) Native American to psychiatrist: "I don't know what it is, Doc, some days I feel like a tee pee and some days I feel like a wig wam."

Psychiatrist: "You know what your problem is? You're two _____."
Clue: He's anxious.

87) During an interview of Winston Churchill on his 87th birthday, a reporter said, "Sir Winston, I hope to wish you well on your 100th birthday." Churchill quipped, "_____ _____."
Clue: There's a turning of the tables here regarding the focus of the reporter's comments.

88) A farmer called the fire department, yelling excitedly: "This is Dave Van Nuck. My barn is on fire. Get out here as quick as you can!"

"OK," said the dispatcher, "but how do we get there?"

Dave paused a moment and said, "Don't you have those _____ any more?"
Clue: The word "how" is ambiguous.

89) President Lincoln was once asked if the press reports regarding a particular issue were reliable. He is said to have answered, "First they _____ and then they re-_____, so I guess that makes them reliable."
Clue: Again, find a second way of interpreting a key word here.

90) Two Eskimos sitting in a kayak got very cold, so they lit a fire in their little boat. The boat sank,

proving once and for all that you can't have your
_____ and _____ too.
Clue: You can't have it all.

91) When Victor Borge (a now-deceased comic
pianist) was asked why the keys of his piano were so
yellow, he insisted that it was not because the piano
was old. It was because "the elephant
_____."
Clue: What causes yellowing of teeth in humans?

92) A woman who was assaulted was brought into the
room to try to identify her attacker. One man in the
police lineup spotted her and said, "That's
_____!"
Clue: There's a kind of reversal operating here.

93) The butcher was waiting on a woman when Mrs.
Bottleson rushed in and said, "Give me a pound of cat
food, quick!"
   Turning to the other customer, who had been waiting
for some time, Mrs. Bottleson said: "I hope you don't
mind my getting waited on before you."
   "Not if you're that _____," quipped the other
customer.
Clue: The implication is that she's not getting the cat
food for her cat.

94) "My wife and I were happy for 25 years."
"Then what happened?"
"We _____."
Clue: Does it say they had 25 happy years of
marriage?

95) Two women are talking. "Do you ever wake up grouchy?"

"No, I usually _____."

Clue: Look for a second interpretation of "wake up."

96) A wife playfully says to her husband, "You need a self-starter to get you up in the morning." Her husband says, "Oh no I don't. Not with a _____ like you around."

Clue: A hostile response. How were the earliest cars started?

97) "I understand your mother-in-law is very ill."

"That's right. In fact, she's in the hospital."

"I'm sorry to hear that. How long has she been in the hospital?"

"Well, in three weeks, it'll be _____."

Clue: He doesn't like his mother-in-law.

98) A man who always has bad luck with the ladies decides to try a more assertive approach. He sees an attractive woman in a bar, buys her a drink, chats a while, then smiles, and with a wink, drops his hotel room key into her purse. He waits an hour, for the sake of appearances, and then goes back to his room. _____ is gone.

Clue: There was no suggestion that the woman reacted positively to him.

99) Trying to talk to him is like trying to take a sip out of a _____.

Clue: Exaggerate! Find a situation involving water where it's impossible to take a sip.

100) Woman to her husband: "Honey, the car is
_____."

Husband: "How do you know?"

Wife: "Because it's in the swimming pool."

Clue: None needed.

101) A man known by everyone in the church to be a heavy drinker asks Father O'Mally what scoliosis is. The priest, thinking that this is a good chance to teach him a lesson, says, "Scoliosis is a condition caused by too much drinking and carousing! Why do you ask? Do you have it bad?"

"Oh no, Father," answered the man, "I was just reading in the paper that _____ has it."

Clue: How can you make this embarrassing to the priest, given what he just said?

102) Little Bobby swallowed a penny. "Quick," shouted his mother, "Call a doctor!"

"Doctor, schmocter!" shouted his father. "Call the rabbi. He can get _____ out of _____!"

Clue: Think more broadly than this particular penny.

103) How to you convert a "man of gold" into a "man of God?"

"Knock the _____ out of him."

Clue: Look at the words "gold" and "God." How do they differ?

104) What did the agnostic dyslexic have to say about religion?

"There is no _____!"

Clue: What would he say about God?

105) Why didn't the maharishi accept Novocain when he went to the dentist? Because he prefers to transcend

_____.

Clue: What kind of meditation did the maharishi Mahesh Yogi do? Play with the term used for this meditation.

106) "Operator, this is Reverend Thomas in Boston. I'd like to place a call to Reverend Pearson in Los Angeles."

"Will you speak with anyone else who answers?"

"No, make it _____ to _____."

Clue: A particular kind of phone call that requires an operator's assistance (and think of another word for a minister).

107) "_____! _____! _____!" said one monk to another. "Is that all you ever think about?"

Clue: It sounds just like a familiar phrase. What term is used to refer to a religious group having views that differ from those of the parent organization?

108) Jim Baker (the once-jailed TV evangelist) wrote a book based on his experiences in the late 1980s. It's called "Do clergy do more than _____ people?"

Clue: What do you call someone who is not associated with the church?

Extra Clue: It's sexual.

109) What do you call a monkey in a minefield? A(n)

_____.

Clue: This kind of monkey starts with a "b."

110) Young son: Dad, I heard that in some parts of Africa, a man doesn't even know his wife before he marries her.

Dad: That _____, son.

Clue: Dad is implying that there are always surprises after you're married.

111) How many Zen masters does it take to screw in a light bulb?

Two. One to _____ and one not to _____.

Clue: Yin and Yang.

112) A 70-year-old woman went to see her doctor with the following complaint: "I don't know what is doctor, I just don't seem to have the desire for sex that I used to have."

The doctor answered, "Well, that's understandable for a woman your age. When did you first notice this?"

"Well, _____."

Clue: Remember, the stereotype is that all 70-year-old women have lost interest in sex. Exaggerate, in the opposite direction.

113) A father and his son were disappointed by the lethargy of the expensive bull they just bought. So they called in the vet, who came by while the son was at school. When he got home, his father told him that the vet had rubbed the bull's gums with a yellow ointment. And the bull, having kicked down his stall, was in the process of mating with every cow in the herd.

"Fantastic!" said the son. "What was in the ointment?"

"Don't know," said Pa, "but it had a vanilla
_____."

Clue: It may take a minute to see this one. If it had that effect on the bull …

114) How do you tell the sex of a chromosome?
   Pull down its _____.
Clue: Think of a variation of "Pull down its pants."

115) A man says to his good friend, "I never knew what happiness was until I got married, and
_____."
Clue: He's not really happy in his marriage.

116) Unhappy husband after a quarrel: "You know, I was a fool when I married you." Wife: "I know, but I was in love _____."
Clue: She gets even with her remark. How can you quickly turn the tables in the interpretation of his own words?

117) Old lawyers never die, they just lose their
_____.
Clue: What do lawyers file when they're dissatisfied with the outcome of a trial?

118) Two fish are in a tank. One turns to the other and says, "Do you know how to _____ this thing?"
Clue: There's no water in this tank.

119) Sign at Adam and Eve's house: "We're never
_____."
Clue: Play with the word used to indicate that you're
open for business 24 hours a day.
Extra Clue: What did Adam and Eve not wear?

120) Sing on front door of music store: "Gone
_____, back in a _____."
Clue: A play on a familiar phrase. Each missing word
distorts a familiar word. Use the name of a famous
composer (especially associated with the piano).
Extra Challenge: Play with the word "back."

121) Pravda (Pre-Gorbachev) announced a contest in
Moscow for the best political joke. First prize:
_____.
Clue: Political jokes in the pre-Gorbachev years were
not very well-received by party leaders. So the answer
must contain something negative.

122) An American tourist in Moscow (pre-
Gorbachev) is explaining our democratic system: "An
American can stand on the steps of the Capitol
Building and shout: 'The President is a bum!'"
   The Russian says, "But we can do that too. Any
Russian can stand on the steps at the Kremlin and
shout: 'The _____ is a bum!'"
Clue: What the Russian is agreeing to is just the
opposite of what you think he's agreeing to.

123) Soviet newspaper feature (pre-Gorbachev):
"Believe it or _____."

Clue: A play on Ripley's "Believe it or not."
Remember, there was no choice but to accept the Party line.

124) It was so cold last winter (how cold was it?) that I saw a lawyer with his hands _____.
Clue: It's another put-down of lawyers. What are lawyers sometimes of accused of having their hands in?

125) A man lost 82 straight bets trying to pick winners in pro football games. "Why not try hockey?" asked his friend.
   "Hockey?" he answered, "I don't _____ hockey."
Clue: The logic behind the answer is inconsistent with the fact that he's lost his last 82 bets on football.

126) A woman was fired from her job at a frozen orange juice company. They said she just couldn't

_____.
Clue: What term do we use to refer to the nature of the orange juice when it's frozen?

127) Why do cannibals refuse to eat clowns?
   Because they taste _____.
Clue: A word that implies "bad" but has an extra meaning here.

128) (A Classic) "Waiter, what's this fly doing in my soup?"
   "Well, I don't know, sir, but it looks like _____."

Clue: The key word here is "doing."

129) "Waiter, what is this you've served me?"
  "Why that's _____ soup, sir."
  "I'm not interested in what it's _____. I want to know what it is now!"
Clue: Only one kind of soup makes a joke out of this.
Extra Clue: Assume the customer is British.

130) What do you get when you cross a toaster with an electric blanket? A _____ that _____ in the morning.
Clue: What do a lot of people have difficulty doing in the morning when they wake up? And what is a prominent feature of toasters?

131) What do you get when you cross a freeway with a bicycle? _____.
Clue: This joke violates the usual pattern of cross jokes. If you wanted to trick someone after a series of cross jokes, what answer might you give here? Treat "cross" as a pun.

132) What does a grape say when you step on it? Nothing. It just gives a little _____.
Clue: Think of a young child who's upset.

133) How do you get down from an elephant? You don't
_____.
Clue: Find an answer based on a pun here.

134) How can you tell when an elephant is getting ready to charge?

He takes out his _____.

Clue: No clue necessary. Many elephant jokes follow this formula.

135) A (fill in any country you want to poke fun at) airplane lands on the runway with great difficulty. As they taxi, the pilot says, "My God! That's the shortest runway I've ever seen!"

"You're not kidding," says the copilot, looking out his window. "But it sure is _____."

Clue: If it's a normal airport, what kind of absurd confusion is possible here?

136) May your future happiness and success be like Ireland's capital—always _____.

Clue: Increasing. What is Ireland's capital?

137) What do you call a real dude in the Navy?

_____.

Clue: Use the word for underwater boats. Think of a word that means "emotionally down."

138) "Did you ever see the Catskill Mountains?"

"No, but I've seen _____."

Clue: No clue necessary.

139) "What happened to Johnny when he fell through the screen door?"

"He got a _____ muscle."

Clue: What are screens (not screen doors) sometimes used for?

140) What's the difference between a cat and a comma?

A cat has _____ at the end òf its _____ , and a comma has a _____ at the end of its _____ .
Clue: All the key words sound like "flaws."

141) A concerned Mr. Goldfarb tells his wife that the doctor said he'd contracted a bad case of gonorrhea. His wife goes to the dictionary and looks the word up.

"Not to worry," she says, "it says right here that it's an inflammation of the _____ ."
Clue: She misunderstood a key word. Remember, she's Jewish. What do you call someone who's not Jewish?

142) An elderly man with a hearing problem suddenly goes deaf in one ear. He goes to a doctor, who pulls a suppository out of his ear. "Here's the trouble," says the doctor.

The old man sighs in relief. "Now I know what I did with my _____ ."
Clue: There's only one possible source of confusion here for someone who's hard of hearing.

143) Why do (fill in any nationality you want to put down) male doctors always make lousy lovers?

They always wait for the _____ to go down.
Clue: A familiar phrase used in connection with certain injuries.

144) A couple of guys from the big city are out in the woods pheasant hunting for the first time. Suddenly, one of them just falls over. He's not moving, and his

eyes are rolled back in his head. So the other guy whips out his cell phone and calls 911. He gasps to the operator, "My friend just fell over and died! What should I do?"

The operator says in a calm voice, "Just take it easy. I can help. First, let's make sure he's dead."

There's silence for a few moments, but then a shot is heard. The guy's voice comes back on line. He says, "_____?"

CLUE: How could the operator's instructions be misinterpreted?

145) "I hear the company president's wife is gonna ask for a divorce."

"Really? Why?"

"She claims he's not _____ what he's doing to the company."

Clue: It's sexual. It's also a negative statement about how he's leading the company.

146) Friend: "How'd you come out in the argument with your wife?"

Husband: "Oh, she came crawling to me on hands and knees."

Friend: "Is that so?"

Husband: "Yes." She said, "Come out from _____ _____."

Clue: He's being literal, and he lost the argument.

147) My wife and I have our differences. But like a Californian after an earthquake, we always say, "With all your _____, I love you still."

Clue: San Andreas.

148) A nudist camp tried to recruit new members by advertising a special: "Only _____ for new members."

Clue: Play with a familiar phrase used in sales. But remember, it's a nudist camp.

149) A visitor to New Mexico was struck by how dry everything looked. "Don't you ever get any rain here?" he asked a local.

The resident thought, and then asked, "Do remember the story about Noah and the Ark, and how it rained for 40 days and 40 nights?"

"Of course I do," said the visitor.

"Well that time, we _____."

Clue: The technique used here is exaggeration (in a negative direction).

150) Bumper sticker: Old mailmen never die. They just lose their _____.

Clue: Synonym for zest or energy.

Extra Clue: What goes at the end of an address on a letter?

151) A lawyer had a jury trial in a very difficult business case. The client had attended the trial, but was out of town when the jury returned its decision, which was for the lawyer and his client. The lawyer immediately sent a telegram to his client, saying, "Justice has triumphed!" The client wired back, "_____ at once!"

Clue: You have to reverse an assumption you've made. What if the client knew he was guilty?

152) What happens when you cross a Mafia don with a lawyer? You have someone who makes you an offer you can't _____.
Clue: You probably know the familiar phrase about the Mafia. What have you always noticed about legal forms?

153) A man and his wife are new arrivals, and are exploring the wonders of Heaven. It was so much fun that the man turned to his wife and said, "See if you hadn't started that _____, we could have _____!"
Clue: He wishes he had died earlier. Something she did extended his life.

154) A woman rushes into her house and yells to her husband, "Sam, pack your things! I just won the lottery!"
   He says, "Shall I pack for warm or cold weather?"
   She answers, "I don't care, as long as you're _____ by tonight."
Clue: She has no intention of sharing it with him.

155) Did you hear that NASA has established a new restaurant on the moon? It has great food, and low prices, but no _____.
Clue: Think of another way to say "The ambiance is poor."

156) A woman who wanted to improve her self-concept went to a bookstore and asked the manager where the _____ section was. The manager

said, "If I told you, that would defeat the whole purpose."
Clue: The joke itself contains all the clues you need (but you will need to think about it a bit).

157) People are like tea bags. You have to put them in _____ before you know how _____ they are. (This is not funny, but the double meanings are there.)
CLUE: What's the natural thing to do with a tea bag?

158) A woman went to the Post Office to buy stamps for her Christmas cards. "What denomination?" asked the clerk. "Oh, good heavens! Have we come to this?" she said. "Well, give me 30 _____ and 30 _____ ones."
Clue: "Denomination" is the key word.

159) At an international medical conference, an American, British and Russian doctor were discussing the limitations of their diagnostic procedures. "It's very sad," said the American, "we treat people for cancer and they die of AIDS." The Brit says, "I know what you mean. We treat them for yellow fever, and it turns out they had malaria. Then, of course, they die." "That is not a problem in our country," said the Russian doctor. "When we treat people for a disease, they die of _____ disease."
Clue: The implication is that they're really not good doctors—or that their treatments are deficient.

160) A family's barn burns down, and the wife calls the insurance company. She says, "We had that barn insured for $50,000, and we want our money!" The

insurance agent says, "Whoa, wait a minute. It doesn't work like that. We'll ascertain the value of the old barn and provide you with a new barn of comparable worth." The wife thinks for a moment and says, "If that's the way you operate, I'd like to cancel the policy on my _____."
Clue: She's not very happy with her marriage.

161) A city doctor decided to start a practice in the countryside. One day he had to go to a farm to see a sick farmer. After a few house calls, he stopped coming to the farm. The puzzled farmer finally phoned him to ask why he stopped coming. The doctor said, "It's your ducks! Every time I come over there, they verbally insult me."
   Question: How do they do this?
Clue: This one is tricky and will take a minute. Don't give up on it.
Extra Clue: What sound does a duck make?

162) Doctors at a local hospital are on strike and are picketing outside the hospital. Hospital officials say they will find out what the doctors' demands are as soon as they can get a _____ over there to _____ the picket signs.
Clue: The doctors made the signs themselves.
Extra Clue: What are doctors famous for? It concerns their writing.

163) Everyone has a photographic memory. Some people just don't have _____.
Clue: What's the one essential thing you need to take a photograph?

164) A Freudian slip is when you say one thing but mean _____.

Clue: It's a play on a familiar phrase. According to Freud, who has the most impact on our early development?

165) A mother takes her seven-year-old son to the doctor. The boy says, "It hurts when I press here (pressing his side), and when I press here (pressing the other side), and here (pressing his leg), and here, here and here (pressing his other leg and both arms)."

   The doctor examined him all over and finally discovered what was wrong. He had a broken _____."

Clue: It hurt when the boy pressed in all those places, but was it clearly stated just where the pain was?

166) A woman is trying to board a bus, but her skirt is too tight and she can't step up. She reaches behind her and lowers her zipper a bit and tries again. The skirt's still too tight. She reaches behind her and lowers the zipper some more. She still can't step up and lowers the zipper a third time. Suddenly, she feels two hands on her derriere, trying to push her up onto the bus. She spins around and says very indignantly, "Sir, I do not know you well enough for you to do that."

   The man responds, "Lady, I don't know you well enough for you to _____ three times either.

Clue: She couldn't actually see her zipper. Everybody makes mistakes.

167) A couple was having a discussion of family finances. The husband finally exploded, "If it weren't for my money, the house wouldn't even be here!"

   The wife answered, "Honey, if it weren't for your money, _____."
Clue: She didn't marry him for love.

168) A distraught man tells his doctor, "Doc, it's finally happened! I've lost my memory! You've gotta help me."

   The doctor asks, "When did you first notice this?"

   The man looks at him and says,
"_____?"
Clue: If he's really lost his memory …

169) A woman's husband has been slipping in and out of a coma for several weeks, and yet she stays at his bedside every single day. When he finally comes to, he motions for her to come nearer. He says, "You know what? You've been with me through all the bad times. When I got fired, you were there for me. When my own business failed, you were there. When I got shot, you were by my side. When we lost the house, you gave me support. When my health failed, you were still by my side. When I think about it now, I think you _____."
Clue: It's the opposite of what you're thinking. In his weakened state, he's seeing a pattern of associations.

170) A woman complains to a friend, "My husband just can't be trusted. He cheats so much that I'm not even sure this baby I'm carrying _____."

Clue: She's not very bright. He's also not the only cheater.

171) An 85-year-old man finally invests in a hearing aid after becoming nearly deaf. It's the new tiny invisible kind that fits right into your ear. Two weeks later on his follow-up visit, his doctor asks how the hearing aid is working out.

"Oh, it's great says the old man. I'm hearing sounds I haven't heard in years."

"And how does your family like it?" asks the doctor.

"Oh," he says, "they don't even know about it yet. Am I having a great time! I've _____ three times in the last two months."

Clue: He's heard some negative things being said about him. If it's negative enough, what might that lead an old man to do?

172) A couple comes to a wishing well. The wife leans over, makes a wish and throws in a penny. The husband decides to make a wish too. But he leans over too far, falls into the well and drowns. The wife is stunned for a while, but then comes to her senses and says, "It _____!"

Clue: She is not upset. You probably made a false assumption about the kind of wish that she made.

173) There are three kinds of people, those who can count _____.

Clue: Assume that the person saying this can't count.

174) COGITO ERGO SPUD. I think, therefore I _____.

Clue: A particular kind of potato. It's orange.

175) During the Clinton Presidency, what was the difference between the White House and a hotel? In the White House the guest was expected to leave a _____ on the pillow.
Clue: What do fine hotels often put on your pillow before bedtime?

176) A Catholic Church's air conditioning system broke down, so they hired a man to crawl a round in the ducts and figure out what was wrong. As he peeked out through a vent in the sanctuary, he saw little old Mrs. Murphy kneeling at the altar saying her rosary. As a joke, he said, in the most authoritative voice he could muster, "This is Jesus. Your prayers will be answered."

The little old lady didn't even blink. She just kept saying her prayers. The man decided she didn't hear him, so he said even louder, "This is Jesus. Your prayers will be answered."

Again, she didn't react. So, mustering all the energy he could, he boomed out, "THIS IS JESUS CHRIST, THE SON OF GOD! YOUR PRAYERS WILL BE ANSWERED!"

She looked up and said, "BE QUIET! I'M TALKING TO _____!"
Clue: She reacts as if she's talking to a child.

177) When everything's coming your way, you know you're in the _____.
Clue: Think of driving on the interstate.

178) What do you call cattle with a great sense of humor? _____.
Clue: This pair of words is sometimes used for people, ideas or projects that are objects of ridicule; i.e., they're laughed at.

179) I was married to Sam for three months, and I had no idea he drank until one night when he came home _____.
Clue: It just the opposite of what you're thinking.

180) How is homework like a juicy steak? It's _____ done.
Clue: Homework is often not done.

181) When an alligator goes on welfare, what does he get? _____.
Clue: A kind of drink.

182) What does Clark Kent use to keep the sun out of his eyes? A _____.
Clue: A boss or manager.

183) A scientist cloned himself, and the experiment produced a duplicate who used very foul language. The clone cursed and swore so much that the scientist finally could take no more. He pushed him out the window, and the clone fell to its death. Later that day, the scientist was arrested for making an obscene _____.
Clue: The allusion here is to telephoning someone.

184) What do you get when you toss a bomb into a kitchen in France? Linoleum _____.
Clue: The most famous French military figure.

185) What's the difference between a Roman barber and an angry circus performer? One's a _____ Roman and the other is a _____ showman.
Clue: The two words rhyme with "paving."

186) Fairbanks, Alaska passed a law outlawing all dogs in public spaces. The city soon became known as _____ Fairbanks.
Clue: Movie star in the 1930's. Play with his first name.

187) What is a zebra? The biggest _____they make.
Clue: Women's clothing.

188) What do you get when you cross an elephant with a skin doctor? A _____ dermatologist.
Clue: A non-ruminant hoofed mammal. (How's that for a useless clue?)

189) What do Eskimos get from sitting on the ice too long? _____.
Clue: Camera.

190) What do you call four Mexican bull fighters trapped in quicksand? _____.
Clue: This is a little silly. Count to five in Spanish. What are the last two numbers?

191) What do you get when you cross a snowman with a vampire? _____.
Clue: What do mountain climbers often suffer from when in the harsh cold too long?

192) Change is inevitable, except from a
_____.
Clue: It costs 75 cents, but you put in a dollar.

193) A woman has identical twins, but has to give them up for adoption. One goes to a family in Egypt, and they name him "Amal." The other goes to a family in Spain, and they name him "Juan." Four years later, Juan's adoptive parents send a photo of Juan to the mother. Upon receiving the picture, she tells her husband she wishes she also had a photo of Amal. Her husband responds, "But they're twins; if you've seen Juan _____."
Clue: A familiar phrase. If they're identical … Play with the sound of the names.

194) A man entered a local paper's pun contest. He sent in his ten best puns, hoping that one of the puns would win. But to his great disappointment, no pun
_____.
Clue: What do people often say when they say a pun accidentally?

195) A neutron goes into a bar and asks, "How much for a beer?" The bartender says, "For you, no
_____."
Clue: What is the definition of a neutron?

196) Two atoms are walking down the street and they run into each other. One says to the other, "Are you all right?"

"No, I'm not. I lost an electron."

"Are you sure?"

"Yes, I'm _____."

Clue: He's certain of it. Find another word for certain.

197) A doctor always stopped off for a hazelnut daiquiri at his favorite bar on the way home. Being a regular, the bartender knew his habits and always had his drink waiting when he walked in at 5:15 p.m. One day, he noticed at 5 p.m. that he was out of hazelnut extract. Thinking quickly, he threw together a daiquiri made from squashed hickory nuts and set it on the bar. The doctor came in and took one sip and said to the bartender, "This isn't a hazelnut daiquiri!"

"I'm sorry," said the bartender, "I ran out of hazelnut. It's a _____, doc."

Clue: The mouse ran up the clock.

198) Two boll weevils grew up together in South Carolina. One went to Hollywood and became a famous actor. The other one stayed behind in the cotton fields and never amounted to much. The second one, naturally, became known as the _____.

Clue: Lesser of …

199) If you take an Oriental person and spin him around several times, what does he become?

_____.

Clue: He becomes confused and doesn't think clearly.

200) What do you call a sleepwalking nun?
    A(n) _____.
Clue: She's Catholic.
Extra Clue: Where does the Pope live?
Extra Extra Clue: To wander.

Paul E. McGhee

Answers to Jokes

1) deep down
2) time does he get up
3) Lebanese
4) get her work done
5) cut in
6) thirsty
7) out of you
8) go far
9) the word "no"
10) vulture capitalists
11) trains … mind … minds … train
12) training wheels
13) Laurel and Hardy (other answers also work; e.g., Moe and Curly, of The Three Stooges)
14) bouquet
15) arm
16) another one
17) you're a cab
18) batteries
19) send you the rest
20) the eggs
21) cervix (service)
22) yesterday … forgot to call
23) Two doctors
24) the batteries
25) is getting better
26) wurst (worst) … come
27) make a prophet (profit)
28) go on

29) peanuts
30) baited
31) Hailing
32) small medium at large
33) repeat it
34) asshole
35) I am not! You're doing fine.
36) drinks … electrician
37) in stitches
38) German (or European)
39) lumbar (lumber)
40) no change
41) dark
42) political statement
43) pending
44) A cheeseburger and fries (or another food order)
45) third question
46) lawyer
47) ring the bell … brings me food
48) several cabs … the wrong one
49) acapella
50) short legs
51) Pooched
52) dirty looks
53) Anna (Now aren't you embarrassed? This is a classic kind of tricky kid's riddle.)
54) broom … eight
55) tell you … laughing at
56) knocks on the door … delivers the message
57) retractable beak
58) hippo … sticks … roof of your mouth
59) nervous mailman
60) down

61) poodle
62) him
63) stick to the roof of your mouth
64) upper twenty thousands (or any other number suggesting a nuclear bomb)
65) Nothing … yet
66) the license number
67) 38-short, let out the shoulders and take in the waist
68) herring (or other fish commonly served in a restaurant)
69) trips
70) Any specific older age; e.g., 27 years (or seven months of continuous employment)
71) are they
72) wafer
73) Diary
74) wait
75) don't give any tip at all (of course, you can reverse
     Republican and Democrat here)
76) receptive contras
77) right
78) joint
79) speaking
80) are moving
81) inclination
82) bring us two, please ("two to go," etc.)
83) train
84) didn't get your telegram
85) want to change
86) (too) tents (tense)
87) You might make it, you look healthy

88) red trucks
89) lie … lie
90) kayak (cake) … heat (eat) it
91) smoked too much
92) her all right
93) hungry
94) met (or got married)
95) let him sleep
96) crank
97) a month
98) His luggage (or anything else of value)
99) fire hydrant (or a hose)
100) flooded
101) the Pope
102) money … anybody
103) l (hell)
104) dog
105) dental medication
106) parson to parson
107) Sects! Sects! Sects!
108) lay
109) baboom (baboon)
110) happens in most countries
111) screw in the bulb (in each blank)
112) Last night, and then again this morning
113) taste
114) genes
115) then it was too late (or any other comment that shows that he was happier before he got married)
116) and didn't notice it
117) appeal
118) drive
119) clothed

120) Chopin … minuet
   Extra Challenge: Bach (e.g., Johann Sebastian)
121) 20 years
122) American President
123) else
124) in his own pocket
125) know anything about
126) concentrate
127) funny
128) the back stroke
129) bean … been (pronounced with a British accent)
130) blanket … pops you out of bed
131) Killed
132) wine (whine)
133) get down from an elephant. You get down from a goose.
134) credit card
135) wide
136) Dublin (doubling)
137) Sub dude
138) them kill mice
139) strained
140) claws … paws … pause … clause
141) gentiles
142) hearing aid
143) swelling
144) OK, now what? (Many things will work here, as long as they establish that his buddy shot him to make sure he was dead.)
145) doing to her
146) under that bed, you coward
147) faults
148) 50% off

149) got about an inch (or any other small number)
150) zip
151) Appeal
152) understand
153) healthy cooking … been here 10 years ago (other answers will also work here)
154) out of the house
155) atmosphere
156) self-help
157) hot water … strong
158) Baptist … Lutheran (any others will also work)
159) that
160) husband
161) Ducks quack. What are doctors sometimes accused of being?
162) pharmacist/nurse, etc… read
163) film
164) your mother (another)
165) finger
166) unzip my fly
167) I wouldn't be here
168) Notice what
169) bring me bad luck
170) is his
171) changed my will
172) really works
173) and those who can't
174) yam
175) mint (in this case, it's not chocolate)
176) your mother
177) wrong lane
178) Laughing stock
179) sober

180) rarely

181) Gatorade

182) supervisor

183) clone fall (phone call)

184) blownapart (Napoleon Bonaparte)

185) shaving ... raving

186) dogless (alludes to Douglas Fairbanks)

187) bra

188) pachy

189) Polaroids

190) Quatro sinko

191) Frostbite

192) vending machine (or any other machine that gives change)

193) you've seen Amal (if you've seen one, you've seen 'em all)

194) in ten did (intended)

195) charge

196) positive

197) hickory daiquiri

198) lesser of two weevils (evils)

199) Disoriented

200) Roamin' (Roman)

Stories and Longer Jokes

1) Herb is the lone survivor of a shipwreck, along with his dog. After two days clinging to a floating piece of wreckage, they come upon an island. The island is deserted, but has hundreds of sheep.

Herb has never been attracted to animals, but after a while he gets so lonely and frightened of dying that he finds himself looking longingly at one of the lambs. But as soon as he goes near her, his dog starts barking and chases the lamb away. The next morning, Herb can think of nothing but the lamb. He gets up early, sneaks over to the lamb, and just as he touches her, the dog again runs up yelping loudly, and scares her away.

A week later, Herb and the dog are walking along the beach, and come across a beautiful young woman lying unconscious on the sand. Herb rushes up and gives her mouth-to-mouth resuscitation, and after a while, she comes to. "Where am I? What happened?"

"You must have survived the shipwreck," he says. "You were unconscious, but I guess I got to you in time."

"Oh, I just don't know how I can thank you," she says, giving him a long tender kiss and pushing her body up against his. "Please let me show my appreciation to you in some way. Just tell me how I can please you. I'll do anything you want."

"Well," says Herb, "there is something. Would you mind _____?"
Clue: If it's what he'd normally say here, it wouldn't be a joke. Think back to the rest of the story. What about the sheep? How can he deal with the dog?

2) A man in his 70s has a woman half his age fall hopelessly in love with him. He says, "I can't marry you, my dear. Father and mother are against it."

She's startled. "What? At your age, your parents are still living?"

"No," he explains, "I mean father ____ and mother ____."
Clue: Think of two familiar two-word expressions consistent with the idea that this marriage wouldn't work very well.

3) A boy is pulling his wagon down the street when the wheels fall off. "I'll be damned!" he says, and puts the wheels back on.

A couple of minutes later, the wheels fall off again. "I'll be damned!" says the boy, and puts them on again.

This time a priest overhears him. "You shouldn't swear like that son," he says. "If those wheels fall off again, just say, 'Praise the Lord!'"

Just then, the wheels do fall off again. "Praise the Lord!" says the boy. And the wheels just roll back to the wagon and attach themselves.

"_____!" says the priest.
Clue: You don't expect this from a priest. But it makes sense here. What did the boy say?

4) A rabbi gets caught in a rainstorm and ducks into a Chinese restaurant to wait it out. At the bartender's invitation, he takes a seat and accepts a complimentary Mai Tai.

Shortly, the rabbi, who usually does not drink alcohol, leans over and punches the bartender in the face. "That's for Pearl Harbor," says the rabbi.

"Pearl Harbor? Are you crazy? I'm Chinese, not Japanese."

"Ach, Japanese, Chinese. What's the difference? But I'm sorry if I offended you. Let me buy you a drink."

The bartender accepts, and a few minutes later leans over and punches the rabbi in the face. "What was that for?" asks the startled rabbi.

"That's for the Titanic!"

"The Titanic? That was destroyed by an iceberg."

"Ah," says the bartender, shrugging his shoulders, "iceberg _____, what's the difference?"

Clue: The clue is "iceberg." What's a common Jewish name? Remember, he wants to get even.

5) A local resident runs over Mrs. Tipson's cat. He knocks on her door and says, "I'm sorry Mrs. Tipson, but I'm afraid I've just run over your cat. But don't you worry, I'll replace him."

"Then don't just stand there. There's a _____ in the kitchen."

Clue: She took him literally. What would the cat do in the kitchen?

6) A woman is conducting a survey on sexual behavior, and she asks an airline pilot, "When was the last time you made love to a woman?"

He answers, "1956."

She is startled and repeats, "1956?"

The pilot adds, "Well, it's only _____."

Clue: Find another way to interpret "1956."

7) The Godfather calls in two of his regular staff and says, "I want a special girl. She has to be exactly 6 feet 6 inches tall, weigh less than 80 pounds, and have red hair."

They look at each other, puzzled, and he says, "Shut your face! Just do it! Bring her to me today, wearing a white sun dress."

All hell breaks loose as they search for this woman, but a call finally comes back: "Godfather, we found someone who has red hair and weighs only 78 pounds, but she's only 6 feet and 3 inches tall. But we could put her in 3-inch heels."

"Bring her to me within the hour," says the Godfather.

The woman arrives shortly, clad in a long white sun dress. The Godfather nods his approval, then goes into the next room and returns with a little red-haired girl in a white sun dress.

He stoops down to the little girl and says: "See what grandpa tells you? If you don't _____ you'll _____."

Clue: He's using the woman to make a point. What do Italian mothers and grandmothers always (stereotypically) try to get their (grand) children to do?

8) A stranger walks into a bar, orders a drink, and then pulls out of his pocket a small toy piano. Then he pulls a mouse out of the other pocket. The mouse sits down at the piano and starts playing the most amazing ragtime piano you ever heard.

The bartender is dumfounded. He says, "Hey, that's great!" Then the man takes a canary out of another pocket, and sets him on the piano. And the canary starts warbling all the songs the mouse is playing. The bartender is even more impressed. So he offers the man $5,000 for the act, and the man takes it.

On the way out, another man calls the stranger aside, and says, "You made a big mistake selling that act for $5,000. You could have gone all over the world and made hundreds of thousands of dollars."

And the stranger says, "Naw, I don't think so. People don't realize it, but that canary can't sing a note. The mouse is a _____."
Clue: This makes the act even more incredible than before. Who were Edgar Bergen and Charlie McCarthy?

9) My grandmother lived to be 99. One day I asked her, "What's your secret?" She told me, "I just make myself get out of bed every morning." So I thought, "Well, that's not too tough, but how do you make yourself get up?"

She said, "It's easy. I just
_____ before I go to bed."
Clue: This is something that would really work and makes sense, even in a non-joking way. What could you do the night before that would leave you no choice but to get out of bed?

10) There was a woman who came in every day to see her doctor in a Health Maintenance Organization. There was nothing wrong with her, but everyone listened patiently and actually looked forward to her visits. One day she didn't show up. She even missed the day after that. When she came in the next day, everyone asked, "Where were you the last two days? We missed you."

She said, "To tell you the truth, _____."
Clue: It's just the opposite of the explanation you expect in this particular situation, although it fits what we generally say in circumstances like this.

11) A man is told by his doctor that he only has 12 hours to live, and when he gets home his wife asks him, "What would you like to do?" And he says, "Make love." So they go into the bedroom and make passionate love.

A couple of hours later, they come out of the bedroom, and she asks him, "Well, you've got 10 hours left, what would you like to do?" And he says, "Make love." So they go at it again.

Then she asks, "Well, you've got 8 hours left, what would you like to do?" Once more he says, "Make love." And she says, "That's easy for you to say, you _____ _____."
Clue: A remark that suggests he's being inconsiderate, and that would be appropriate in any other context other than this one. It's a phrase we sometimes use when we're up late.

12) A man (give him the identity of anyone you want to put down) goes ice fishing. He cuts a hole in the ice

but then hears a loud voice say, "There are no fish there!"

Although startled at this, he moves over to another location and begins cutting a new hole. Again, a voice booms, "There are no fish there!"

He tries a new spot, and the voice repeats, "I said there are no fish there!"

"Who is that?" he cries out. "Who's talking to me?"

"The _____," says the voice.

Clue: It's not God. In this joke, you're trying to make the person look stupid. So think of a situation where there's ice, but where there couldn't possibly be fish below.

13) A speaker says to his audience, "We've all heard the phrase, 'Nobody's perfect'. But if there's anyone here who thinks he or she is perfect, just raise your hand, because I'd really like to meet a perfect person."

No one raises their hand at first. But then he notices a middle-aged man way in the back waving his hand back and forth. "Great!" says the speaker, "We've finally found a perfect person. Tell me sir, are you really perfect?"

"No, no, no," said the man, "I'm raising my hand for my _____."

Clue: It's someone else. But who? What bad habit do previously-married couples often have when annoyed with their new spouse?

14) An avid golfer hooks his ball into the woods and goes searching for it. While looking, he comes across a leprechaun who is brewing a strange concoction in a

small pot. "Whatever are you making?" asks the golfer. "It smells great!"

"It's a magic brew," says the leprechaun. "If you drink it, you'll become such a good golfer that you'll never again be defeated."

"Well, let me have a drink of it then," says the golfer.

"As you wish," says the leprechaun, "but I must warn you that it has a serious side effect. It will sharply lower your sexual desire."

"I can live with that," says the golfer, taking half a dozen big gulps. And sure enough, the golfer never loses another game. Within six months, he's declared regional champion. He's so delighted with this that he goes back to the woods to thank the leprechaun. "It worked," he says. "I'm the best golfer anyone's ever seen around here."

"Yes, but how's your sex life?" asks the leprechaun.

"Pretty good," says the golfer. "I've had sex three or four times in the last six months."

"That doesn't sound very good to me," says the leprechaun.

"Well," says the golfer, "It's not that bad for a _____ _____."

Clue: There's no trick here. Just think of someone who you don't expect to have sex very often—if at all.

15) The Episcopal Church assigns a woman pastor to a small-town parish. The women like her, but the men have their doubts. She likes to fish, so when the men get together a fishing party, she asks to go along.

The men are so distracted by her presence in the boat that they get to the middle of the lake and discover they left the bait on the dock.

The pastor says, "Well, there's no sense in us all going back. Wait here." And she climbs out of the boat and walks across the water back to the dock.

One of the men says, "Isn't that typical? They send a woman pastor to a fishing town, and she can't _____ _____."

Clue: This remark would normally make sense, but it completely overlooks the incredible feat of walking on water.

16) In the early Gorbachev years, a firm sends a man to the USSR to close a deal. He's convinced they'll be spying on him. The Soviets put him in a fine hotel, but he knows it has to be bugged. He searches for hours and finally finds it under the bed—a plate attached to the floor with a single nut. He quickly disassembles it and goes to sleep. The next morning, the desk clerk asks if he noticed anything unusual or had any trouble during the night.

"No, not at all, why?"

"The people in the room under you did. Early this morning, _____."

Clue: What if the thing he disconnected wasn't a bug, but a functional part of the building?

17) The time has come for St. Peter's annual 3-week vacation, so Jesus volunteers to fill in for him at the Pearly Gates. "It's no big deal," explains St. Peter. "You just sit here at the registration desk and ask each

person a little about his or her life. Then send them up to housekeeping to pick up their wings."

In the second week, Jesus looks up to see a tired-looking old man in front of him. "I'm a simple carpenter," explains the old man. "But I once had a son. He was born in a very special way and was unlike anyone else in the world. He went through a great transformation, even though he had holes in his hands and feet. He was taken from me a long time ago, but his spirit lives on forever. People tell his story all over the world."

"Father!" Jesus cries out. "It's been so long!"

The old man squints, stares for a moment, and says, "_____?"

Clue: It wouldn't be a joke if it were really God. Who else fits the bill?

18) Lenny is selling Sal, a good buddy, a suit. "I'm telling you Sal, you get a quality suit like this and even your best friend won't recognize you. Just take a walk outside a bit and get the feel of it."

Sal goes out and returns a few minutes later. Lenny rushes up to him and says, "Good morning _____ _____?"

Clue: This is predictable (although absurd), given what Lenny has just said to Sal.

19) A well-known brain surgeon was taking reporters on a tour of the hospital's new brain transplant facility.

"These," said the doctor, "are secretaries' brains, at $3,000 a pound. And here are some salesperson's, brains, at $8,000 a pound. And these are executives' brains, at $40,000 a pound."

A puzzled reporter interrupted, "Wait, why are the brains of executives so much more?"

"Young man," said the doctor, "do you realize how many _____?"
Clue: Look for some kind of reversal of the assumptions you're making here.

20) Back in the old west, an Irishman, an Italian, and a Chinese decide to become partners and start a mining operation. The Irishman runs the office, the Italian is general foreman, and the Chinese is in charge of supplies.

The mine quickly becomes successful, but the Chinese is missing. Fearing foul play, the other two partners search the storehouse, and then the mine— nothing!

Finally, in the most remote part of the mine, just as they are about to give up in despair, the Chinese partner jumps out of the shadows with a big smile on his face, and shouts, "_____!"
Clue: Remember, he's Chinese. And what is he in charge of? Also, what peculiarities of sound occur when Chinese speak English?

21) One day a man was startled to find God talking to him: "I have big plans for you. Prepare!"

So he went out and got a facelift, a hair transplant, liposuction, contact lenses, and a new wardrobe. On the way home, he was run over by a bus and found himself standing in front of the Throne. "If you had such big plans for me, Lord, why did you let me get hit by a bus?"

The Lord shrugged, "I didn't _____."

Clue: You need to reject the assumption that the Lord knows everything. Remember, the man made a lot of changes in his appearance.

22) Back in 1985, the Pentagon had just developed a new computer that could understand and answer human voice commands. Suddenly, an alarm sounds, lights start flashing, and a synthetic computer voice says, "The Soviet Union has launched a nuclear attack."

One of the generals shouts to the machine: "Is the attack coming from land, sea, or air?"

"Yes," answers the computer.

"Yes, what?" screams the general.

"Yes, _____!" answers the computer.

Clue: What is always expected when addressing a superior officer?

23) It was early afternoon, and the boss—Mr. Condon—announced that he was going home early for the weekend. All of his employees were sure that he was going to play golf and wouldn't be calling in, so they all left too after a while.

But when Sam, the accountant, came home, he found Mr. Condon in bed with his wife. So he quietly slipped out and went to a movie.

The next Friday, Mr. Condon again announced that he was going home early. And all the employees again started leaving—except for Sam. "What's the matter, Sam?" someone asked. "You can leave. He won't be back."

"I know," replied Sam, "but I left early last week, and almost _____."

Clue: His reaction to what happened the week before reflects a concern that is just the opposite of what you'd expect. What should the boss be concerned about in this situation?

24) A well-known Mafia figure being tried for murder bribes one of the jurors to hold out for manslaughter—forever, if necessary. The jury is out for 29 hours and finally returns a verdict of manslaughter. After the trial, the defendant says to the bribed juror, "Listen, I appreciate that! Did you have any trouble?"

"I'll say I did," he answers. "I had a really tough time of it. I held out for manslaughter, just like you asked. Everyone else wanted _____."
Clue: It wouldn't be funny if the answer was "murder."

25) Some years ago, there was a congressman who went to a reservation of Native Americans to speak to a large group in his district. "My good friends, I shall see to it that the government helps you."

"Oom galla!" shouted the audience.

"I shall see to it that you have better schools."

"Oom galla!" they shouted again.

"I will work for better housing for you and jobs for those who want them."

"Oom galla!"

"I will see to it that you get federal grants."

"Oom galla! Oom galla!"

After his speech, he was chatting with some of the elders about their problems, when he suddenly noticed some very handsome prize bulls grazing in a meadow nearby. He said, "They're really spectacular animals. Do you mind if I walk over and have a closer look?"

"OK," said the chief, "but be careful you don't step in the _____."

Clue: You shouldn't need a clue for this one. An often-heard expression when you don't believe or trust someone.

26) In a public park one night, a beautiful male statue and a lovely female statue were miraculously given life by a good fairy. After sitting motionless in the park for 35 years, they were alive! She looked at him, and he looked at her. And they knew what had to be. Hand in hand, the two former statues disappeared behind a large bush. Sounds of laughter and great joy came from behind the bush. Squeals of delight and pleasure were heard throughout the night. A passerby snuck a look behind the bush and couldn't believe his eyes. The two former park statues were

_____ _____.

Clue: It's not what you think! It concerns pigeons. Remember, they used to be statues.

27) Quasimodo advertises for a man to ring the bells. The next day, a man comes in with no arms. "Are you kidding?" says Quasimodo.

"I'm serious," says the man. "I need the job. Just give me a chance."

"OK," says Quasimodo, "ring the bells. After all, who am I to discriminate against the handicapped?"

So the man runs up the stairs, takes a flying leap at one of the bells and rings it with his head—boing!— and collapses in a heap. Then he picks himself up, takes a run at the second bell—boing! But as he runs at the third bell, he completely misses it, flies out the window and falls to his death below.

A crowd gathers around the body, and when Quasimodo comes down, they ask him, "Who was this man?"

"Well, I never knew his name," he replies, "but his face _____."
Clue: A familiar phrase for situations where we recognize someone but can't remember their name.

28) The next day, another man with no arms applies for the bell-ringing job. Quasimodo says, "Amazing! I had a guy come in here yesterday that looked just like you."

"I know," says the man. "That was my brother."

"Listen," says Quasimodo, "this is dangerous work for a man with no arms. Look what happened yesterday."

But the man refuses to leave, so Quasimodo eventually gives in and lets him ring the bells. But exactly the same thing happens. The first two leaps at the bell are ok, but on the third, the man flies out the window and falls to his death.

Again, when Quasimodo comes down they say, "Who was this man?"

"I never knew his name," says Quasimodo, "but he's a _____ for his brother."
Clue: Again, find a familiar phrase that fits the situation.

29) Back in the old west, two New Yorkers hear about the war between the settlers and a tribe of Native

Americans called the Caringees. Since the Caringees were killing all settlers in sight to win back their lands, the government was offering a $1,000 bounty on the heads of all Caringees brought in—dead or alive. The New Yorkers decide to head out west in order to cash in.

During their first night on the range in Caringee territory, they fall asleep dreaming of the possibilities for riches. The next morning, one of them wakes up to discover that they are surrounded by hundreds of Caringees. He pokes his partner and shouts, "Wake up! Wake up! We're _____!"

Clue: The punch line assumes they think they are in control of the situation.

30) An American psychiatrist was touring the UK and visited a home for the dangerously insane. There were many sad cases, but he noticed one man laying colored bricks in lovely mosaic patterns in the garden. "That's beautiful!" he said to the worker.

"Thanks, I built it all myself."

"Where's your studio?"

"I don't have a studio. I'm a patient here."

"A patient? Good heavens man, you're an artist! When I get back to London, I'll call the director and have you paroled. I know many wealthy Londoners who'll commission you to design one of these for their garden. You'll be wealthy within a year."

"You'd do this for me?"

"Of course! Well, here's my bus. I'll be in touch."

Just as the psychiatrist is climbing into the bus, something hits him on the head, and he falls back down the steps. After a minute, he looks around to see

what hit him. It's a colored brick. He looks over to
his artist/patient friend, who smiles and says,
"_____!"
Clue: Think of any remark that makes it clear that he
really does belong in the institution.

31) Three businessmen are arrested in a Latin
American country, and sentenced to death by firing
squad. As they were taken out to be shot, the lawyer
says, "They don't look very bright. Let's trick them."

The lawyer was chosen to be shot first. After
"Ready ... Aim ..." he said, "Typhoon!" The firing
squad ran for cover and the lawyer escaped.

The banker tried a similar tactic. "Ready ... Aim
..." and he shouted, "Tidal wave!" Again, everyone
ran for cover and he escaped.

Then it was the salesman's turn. After "Ready ...
Aim..." he screamed, "_____!"
Clue: Think of a disastrous event which would
normally distract people and make the execution less
important, but which would have the opposite of the
intended effect here.

32) An 90-year-old man goes to confession and tells
the priest: "I made love to 3 beautiful women last
weekend."

"For your penance, you should say the Rosary," said
the priest.

"What's that?" said the old-timer. "I'm not
Catholic."

"You're not Catholic? Then what are you telling me
for?"

Said the old timer: "I'm _____!"

Clue: He's not there because he feels he's done something wrong. Remember, he's 90 years old.

33) A banker calls up an optimistic Texas oil man to review his loans. "We loaned you a million dollars to perk up your old wells, and they went dry."

"Coulda been worse," says the oil man.

"Then we loaned you a million to drill new wells, and they were all dry holes."

"Coulda been worse," replies the oil man.

"Then we loaned you another million to buy new equipment, and it all broke down."

"Coulda been worse," says the oil man.

"And I'm tired of hearing that!" snaps the banker. "How could it have been worse?"

The oil man says, "It coulda been _____."
Clue: An answer that suggests that the oil man himself hasn't really been hurt by this at all.
Extra Clue: Whose money was it?

34) An early believer in cryonics was thawed out 50 years later, and began to panic when he realized that he no longer qualified for any kind of job. Then he remembered his investments and called up a broker to check their value. "Thirty million dollars," he was told.

He was beside himself with joy—until the operator said, "Your three minutes are up. Please deposit _____ _____."
Clue: Consider exaggerated inflation.

35) Goldstein, a salesperson, spotted an Arab lying in the sand while driving through the Negev desert. He

rushed over, picked him up, and showed him an exquisite collection of ties. "Are you in luck! I have here the best selection of ties you ever saw."

The Arab whispered, "Water! Water!"

"Look, for you, a special bargain—five dollars."

"No, I need water … please!"

"Well, you drive a hard bargain. Four dollars is the best I can do."

"Pul-eeze, give me some water!"

"Oh, you want water? Well, no problem. If you just head over that dune and turn right in about 1/4 mile, you'll find the Camel Club. They'll give you all the water you want."

So the Arab slowly crawled over the sand dune, and with his last ounce of strength, pulled himself up to the front door of the Camel Club. "Water!" he begged, "Give me some water."

"You want water? You came to the right place. We got well water, seltzer water, whatever kind of water you want. The only thing is you can't get in
_____."

Clue: Look for irony. Why was the salesperson put in the story? .

36) A couple in a large van was driving along when a rabbit suddenly darted across the road. There was no way to avoid it. Splat! They stop and go back to look at it. The husband says, "Well, there's nothing we can do to help him now."

"Yes there is," says the wife. She runs back to the van and comes back with a spray can. She sprays the dead bunny and while they watch, it comes back to its natural form. He gets up and hops across the road, pauses, waves goodbye, hops some more, pauses, waves goodbye, and finally hops into the woods.

"That's incredible!" says the husband. "What's in that can?"

She shows him the label which reads, "_____ restorer with permanent _____."

Clue: A product someone might use if they were bald. You're on your own regarding the wave.

37) In a saloon in the old west, the door swings wide open, and in walks a dog—on its hind legs. He waddles up to the bar and says, "Gimme a whiskey!"

The bartender is enraged and orders the dog out. The dog refuses. So the bartender reaches down, grabs his six-shooter, and shoots the silver dollar right out of the dog's front foot. The dog howls and yips and runs out the door.

The next day, the same dog walks in, this time with a six-gun on each hip. All talk stops as the dog looks slowly around the room and says, "I'm after the man who shot my _____."

Clue: A familiar phrase from westerns.

38) An insurance salesperson tried everything to get a client to buy life insurance, but he wouldn't budge. Finally, in desperation, the salesperson says, "Ok, I've met my match. You're not going to buy. I can accept that. But in consideration of all the time I've spent with you, would you please sign this testimonial letter for me?"

The client reads the letter out loud: "This is to confirm that I will not buy insurance from you regardless of how hard you try to convince me that I should or how good your arguments are."

"What kind of testimonial letter is this?" says the puzzled client. "Even if I did sign the letter, who could you show it to without feeling like a fool?"

The salesperson says, "I'll show it to _____ after _____."

Clue: The first blank is a person. The second describes the conditions under which he would show the letter.

Extra Clue: Under what conditions would this person be annoyed that he didn't buy life insurance?

39) O'Malley owns a store that's just been burglarized. 100 of his best suits were stolen. He meets his friend Kelly on the street. "I'm sorry to hear about the robbery," says Kelly. "Did you lose much?"

"Some," replies O'Malley. "But it would have been much worse if the burglar had broken in the night before."

"Why?" asks his friend.

"Well, you see, the very day of the robbery, I _____ _____."

Clue: It's something he did in the store. What do you often do in order to sell more goods?

40) A terminated employee requested an exit interview with the human resources director of the company.

"I understand you have an issue?"

"An issue of what? I probably didn't read it."

"I mean you wish to protest."

"Well, I'm concerned about the environment, whales, and racial equality, but that's on my own time."

"I was referring to your position here."

"You mean the way I'm sitting?"

"Are you being straight here?"

"My personal life is my own business."

"Just tell me, why did your boss fire you?"

"He wouldn't tell me. That's why I'm here. He just said he couldn't _____ to me."

Clue: This interchange demonstrates the problem.

41) An eccentric corporate president offering a large contract invited all interested competitors to dinner at his estate. After dinner, he took them outside and showed them his swimming pool—filled with hungry alligators. "The contract," he said, "goes to anyone who dares swim the pool from one end to the other."

Out of nowhere, a man jumped in and frantically splashed his way across the pool. He pulled himself out on the far side just inches ahead of the snapping jaws.

"Now that's heroic!" cried the eccentric. "The contract is yours."

"Thank you very much," said the man. "Now show me _____!"

Clue: No one would risk his life just to get a contract.

42) An old man calls in his grandson for a chat. "Johnny, you're thirty years old, single, no babies. We're worried. What's the problem?"

Johnny shrugs, "I haven't met the right woman."

"Ah," says the old man. "And what are you looking for?"

Without speaking, Johnny taps his forehead, then rubs his thumb and fingers together, and finally makes two open-handed gestures over his chest.

The old man nods. "Yes, brains are very important," he says, tapping his head. "And money certainly helps." Then, imitating the two-handed gesture over his chest, he asks, "But why must she have _____?"

Clue: The old man has misunderstood the third gesture. What might an old man think of when two hands are held up in this fashion?

Extra Clue: A medical problem associated with aging.

43) Two friends were out hiking in the forest when suddenly they came across an enormous black bear, seven feet tall! The bear was up on his hind legs, growling in anger.

One of the friends quickly lowered his pack to the ground, pulled out a pair of running shoes, and began lacing them on.

"Don't be ridiculous," said the other. "You can't outrun that bear!"

"I know," said the first, "but I don't have to outrun him, I just have to _____!"

Clue: Put the emphasis on "him," not on "outrun."

44) The star running back of the college football team was about to fail English and flunk out of school. The coach called up the head of the English Department and begged him to give the student one last chance.

"Ok," said the English professor, "send him over."

So the student goes over, and the professor says, "I'll ask you just three questions. Get one of them right, and you pass. First question: How many days of the week begin with the letter 'T'?"

The student mulls it over and says, "Two! Today and tomorrow."

"Let's move on to the next question. How many seconds are there in a year?"

Again, after considerable thought, the running back says, "Twelve! January 2, February 2 …"

"Let's skip right to the third question. Since Christmas is coming soon, tell me how many times the letter 'D' appears in the title of the song 'Rudolph the Red Nosed Reindeer'."

The player squinted and seemed to be running the song title over and over in his mind. Finally, he answered: "Seven!"

"Seven? How did you come up with seven?"

The athlete counted on his fingers as he hummed, "_____."

Clue: What sound do people use when they sing songs without the words?

45) A prominent looking gentleman lost his wallet at a dance. "Excuse me!" he announced standing on a chair, "but I lost my wallet with $600 in it. I'll give $50 to anyone who finds it."

A voice from the rear shouted, "I'll give _____!"
Clue: No clue needed.

46) Sam and Tony owned a clothing store. When Sam returned from vacation, he was startled to walk in and

find his partner walking on crutches and bandaged
from head to toe.

"My God, what happened?" he asked.

"You remember that purple and green checked suit
with the narrow lapels that we've been stuck with for
years? I sold it!"

"So what happened to you? The customer didn't like
the suit?"

"The customer loved the suit," said Tony, "but his
_____ nearly killed me!"

Clue: Who would buy such a suit? He'd have to be
blind.

47) Two gamblers had a run of hard luck and got
stuck in a small town in Montana with virtually no
money. They heard that the hills had a lot of wolves
and that wolf pelts sold for $40 apiece. So they rented
a gun, bought 6 shells and a knife with the last of their
money, and set out for the hills.

They made a little fire and fell asleep as the sun set.
A little later one of them was startled out of his sleep
by a long eerie howl. He looked out at the bushes
around the dying fire and found that they were
surrounded by hundreds of snarling wolves.

He shook his buddy and said, "Wake up, we're
_____!"

Clue: You've already seen this joke in another form.
(Notice how easy it is to make different jokes from the
same punch line.)

48) Carson's beer ran a nation-wide contest for a new
slogan. The top prize was one million dollars.
Thousands of entries came in, and a winner was finally

selected. It stated: "Carson's beer: Like a cabin by the lake." It was the basis for a multi-million dollar ad campaign across the country.

Then Mr. Carson came by the ad agency and asked, "What does it mean? Why is Carson's beer like a cabin by the lake?"

There was immediate panic. No one had thought to ask. They set out to find the contest winner, and asked him, "What does it mean? How is Carson's beer like a cabin by the lake? Just tell us and we'll double the prize."

"Because," he said, "it's about as close as you can get to _____."

Clue: This turns out to be a put-down of the beer. What's a common criticism of some light beers?

49) One day an elderly couple came to a sex therapist and asked him to counsel them on their sexual technique. He did and told them that everything was fine—that they really had no problems.

They paid his $50 fee, but came back again the following week, and the week after that. After the sixth visit, the doctor said, "You two are not only normal, you're very good sexual partners. Why do you keep coming back?"

The man said, "Well, Doc, this kind of thing ain't covered by Medicare, and at $50 a visit you're cheaper than _____."

Clue: They aren't married and need a place to have sex.

50) A man has a fight with his wife, and goes to a bar to cool off. After two beers, he phones home to apologize.

"Hello, honey, it's me. What're you makin' for dinner?"

"What am I makin', you bum? Poison! That's what!"

"Well just make _____! I'm not comin' home."

Clue: How can he turn the tables on her?

51) A man walks into a bar with his dog. The bartender says, "Get out! We don't allow dogs in here."

"Wait a minute," says the man. "This is no ordinary dog. He can talk."

"Sure he can," says the bartender. "If he can talk I'll give you a hundred bucks."

The man puts the dog on a stool and says, "Ok Blackie, what do we call the top part of a house?"

"Roof!"

"Right. And what's on the outside of a tree?"

"Bark!"

"Good. Now let's try something a little tougher. Name a surrealist French sculptor."

"Arp!"

"Terrific! And who would you say is the greatest baseball player of all time?"

"Ruth!"

The bartender is furious. "Listen pal, get that dog out of here before I throw you both out."

As soon as they get out on the street, the dog says, "_____?"

Clue: What if the dog really could talk?

52) A small town barber was widely known for his know-it-all attitude and tendency to put people down. Yet almost everyone liked him. One client had this exchange with the barber:

"Going on vacation this year?"

"Yeah, to Rome."

"Lot of pollution and crime there. But you can always stand in St. Peter's Square and see the Pope."

"Yeah, I'm hoping to get an audience with him."

"You, an audience? The Pope sees kings and presidents. Why would he want to see a small-timer like you?"

"I just hoped I could see him privately."

"Well, forget it. You've got nothing he wants."

A month passes, and the guy is back for a haircut. The barber asks, "How was Rome?"

"Great! I saw the Pope!"

"From St. Peter's Square, of course, with the crowd."

"Yes. But then the darndest thing happened. Two guards pushed their way though the crowd to where I was standing, and one of them says, 'The Pope would like to see you.'"

"So I went along with them right into the Vatican and up to the Pope's private apartment. And there he is, just waiting for me with this big smile on his face."

"I asked him, 'You wanted to see me, Holy Father?'"

"'Yes, I did,' he said. 'I noticed you there in the crowd. Do you mind my asking you a personal question?'"

"Of course not, Holy Father."

"'Fine,' says the Pope, 'I just wanted to know, where did you get that _____?'"
Clue: What's one way to get even with the barber for his constant put-downs? What might the Pope notice about the visitor from his balcony? What is the visitor's link with the barber?

53) A college student received a phone call from his brother Tom back home. "Your cat's dead," said Tom.
   The student fell apart and started crying uncontrollably. "Damn it Tom," said the student, "couldn't you break it to me a little more gently? You could have said, 'Your cat got up on the roof, and we couldn't get it down.' Then you could say, 'It fell as it tried to jump to a tree.' And then you could tell me, 'it died after the fall.'"
   "I'm sorry," said Tom. "You're right. I was crude."
   A couple of weeks later, the student again got a call from Tom, who said, "Grandpa _____."
Clue: Their grandfather has just died.

54) A well known comedian died and woke up in the presence of a man in a white flowing robe. He wondered where he was.
   The man said, "I have examined your life and have decided that you deserve this." He presented the comic with 30 pages of the most beautifully written material he'd ever seen: The Golden Script! There must have been an hour and a half of hilarious material there, with each line funnier than what came before it.
   The comic looked up with tears in his eyes: "So, I'm in Heaven, then?"

"Not exactly," smiled the other. "You've gone the other way."

"Then why have you rewarded me with this wonderful material?" asked the comic.

The man answered, "What are you going to do for _____?"

Clue: What would be real Hell for a comedian?

55) A famous acting teacher was telling her students about the worst actress she'd ever seen. She was so bad, no one would hire her. But then she married a rich producer who included her in all his shows. Once he produced a stage adaptation of *The Diary of Anne Frank*. Her portrayal of Anne was so bad that when the Gestapo came searching for her, the handful of people still in the audience stood up and shouted, "She's _____."

Clue: This is a different kind of humor. How can they get even with her for her bad acting?

56) A conductor on a passenger train was caught throwing people under the wheels of the train when he thought no one was looking. At his trial, he was found guilty of first degree murder and sentenced to die in the electric chair. The judge told him he was a terrible representative of his profession.

On the execution day, he survived three massive jolts of electricity without any apparent injury. "How could this be?" asked the warden.

"Well, like the judge said," sneered the doomed man, "I'm a _____."

Clue: Find a link between electricity and his profession.

57) A country church had a surplus of funds, and the financial committee asked the pastor for a recommendation on how to spend it. The pastor suggested a chandelier. The committee thanked him and began their deliberations. The pastor was later told the request had been denied. He asked why. "Because," the chairman explained, "in the first place, none of us could spell it; in the second place, none of us could play it; and in the third place, what the church really needs is more _____."
Clue: It's precisely what the pastor requested.

58) Frank Perdue (who has his own brand of chicken products in supermarkets) visits the Pope and says, "I'm willing to donate a million dollars to the Catholic Church in exchange for one word."

"What word?" asks the Pope.

"A word in the Lord's Prayer," says Frank. "Just change 'Give us this day our daily bread' to 'Give us this day our daily chicken.'"

"No, I couldn't possibly do that," says the Pope.

"Well, think about it," says Frank.

The next day, Perdue is back. "OK, I'll make it two million dollars if you make it chicken. Not bread. Chicken."

"No, it can't be done," says the Pope.

"Well, think about it," says Frank.

The next day, Frank is back again. "Well, these are my tickets to head back home today. This is your last chance. Five million dollars to your church in exchange for a single word: chicken! Not bread. Chicken!"

The Pope sighs deeply and calls in his top Cardinal. "Yes?" asks the Cardinal. The Pope says, "How firm is our deal with _____?"
Clue: If the Pope had already made a financial deal in connection with The Lord's Prayer and some other product, what product would it be?

59) A newlywed said to his bride, "Every time we make love, I'm gonna put a dollar bill in this metal box." And true to his word, as the months passed, he stuffed a dollar in the box every time they engaged in marital bliss. But the time came when he had to go on a lengthy business trip. He took his wife's picture, and every time he dreamed of making love to her, he mailed her a dollar.

When he arrived home, he said, "Darling, let's see how much we've saved." They opened up the box, and out fell a bunch of $5, $10, and $20 bills. "How is this possible?" he asked. "I only gave you one dollar at a time!"

"Yes, darling," said his wife, "but _____!"
Clue: If money is put in the box only after she makes love, and he only gives her $1 bills, and he's been on a trip …

60) On her death bed, a woman was expressing her final wishes to her husband of many years.
"Dominick, you've been so good to me all these years. I know you never even thought about another woman. Now that I'm going, I want you to marry again as soon as possible, and I want you to give your new wife all my expensive clothes."

"I can't do that darling," he said. "You're a size 16 _____."

Clue: Her assumption about his fidelity is entirely wrong.

61) The patient cleared his throat in embarrassment before explaining his unusual problem. "YOU SEE DOC," he boomed in a voice so deep and raspy that it was hard to understand, "I CAN'T GO ON WITH THIS VOICE ANYMORE—IT'S DRIVING ME CRAZY! CAN YOU FIX IT SO I SOUND LIKE A NORMAL PERSON?"

"I'll certainly try," said the doctor. After examining the patient, he reported that some sort of weight was pulling down on the vocal cords, loudening and distorting the voice. "Any idea what it could be?"

The patient cleared his throat again. "ACTUALLY, DOC, I HAPPEN TO BE ... UH ... ESPECIALLY WELL-ENDOWED, AND MAYBE THAT'S WHAT'S DOING IT! BUT LISTEN, IF YOU HAVE TO REMOVE SOME OF IT, THAT'S OK WITH ME! I'LL DO ANYTHING TO GET A VOICE LIKE A REGULAR GUY!"

So the doctor went ahead with the operation. The patient telephoned two weeks later. "Hey doc," he babbled happily, "I can't thank you enough. I finally sound just like anyone else. I can lead a normal life. It's just great! By the way, doc, what'd you do with the piece of my penis you removed?"

"I _____."

Clue: The exact answer you give here is not as important as the way you say it.

62) Sylvia had lived a wonderful life, having been married four times. Now she waits at the Pearly Gates. St. Peter says to her, "I notice that you first married a banker, then an actor, then a minister, and finally an undertaker. What kind of system is that for the life of a good Christian woman?"

"A very good system." Sylvia replies. "One for _____, two for _____, three to _____, and four to _____!"

Clue: In childhood, you said "On your mark …"

63) A man with terrible financial woes stands on the edge of a bridge poised to jump, when he hears a voice: "Go down to the Casino!"

He obeys the voice and goes down to the Casino. When he gets in, he hears the voice again: "Roll the dice!" He does, and wins—again and again. Each time, the voice says, "Let it ride!" Finally, with over half a million dollars on the table, he realizes his financial troubles are over. As he reaches over to sweep it in, the voice again says, "Let it ride!" Slowly, and reluctantly, he moves it back and promptly loses the whole pile.

"What now!?" he screams out.

"_____," says the voice.

Clue: You don't expect the voice that saved him to now give up on him, but …

64) Before the fall of the Berlin wall, a teacher in an East Berlin school room asks little Hans to give an example of a dependent clause.

"Our cat has a litter of 10 kittens," he answers, "all of which are good Communists."

"That's excellent," says the teacher. "You have a good grasp of grammar, as well as the Party Line."

Several weeks later, a government inspector visits the school and the teacher again calls on Hans.

"Our cat has a litter of 10 kittens," he repeats, "all of which are good Western Democrats."

"That is not what you said a few weeks ago," snapped the teacher with embarrassment.

"Yes," replied Hans, "but the kittens' eyes _____ now."

Clue: Hans has learned some things about Communism he didn't know before. You also need to know a little about how kittens develop in the first few weeks of life to understand this joke.

65) A man who is petrified of flying has to take a business trip. He boards the plane, makes his way to his seat, and gets a strangle hold on both arm rests. A flight attendant sees this and decides to try to comfort him.

"You look nervous," she says. "Do you fly often?"

"No," he answers. "I travel by train. It's safer."

"Well, I don't know about that," she says. I read in the paper just last week about a passenger train going through the desert with nothing around it for a hundred miles. Then, all of a sudden, it derailed and exploded. All the passengers were killed."

"My God!" says the passenger. "What happened?"

"A _____ fell on it," says the stewardess.

Clue: What's the one thing that might fall on the train that would do anything but calm the passenger's anxiety about flying?

66) A man traveling through Northern Ireland had to spend a night in a Belfast hotel. He was told he'd be safe as long as he stayed in his room between sundown and sunrise.

His room had no TV, and there wasn't much to do in the hotel. By 10 p.m., he had read the papers, and was having a nicotine fit. From his window, he could see a small shop at the corner which seemed to be open. He decided to risk it.

He crept down the stairs, out the back door, and just as he approached the shop, he ran smack into a hefty man with a stocking over his head and a gun in his hands. The man asked, "Are you Catholic or Protestant?"

The salesman began to panic, but his thinking was clear. "If I say 'Protestant' and he's I.R.A., it's over. If I say 'Catholic' and he's Protestant, that's no better." So, on an impulse, he says, "I'm _____."

The gunman looks up to Heaven and says, "Allah be praised!"

Clue: No clue necessary. Sometimes the improbable occurs.

67) A man down on his luck looked up to Heaven and said, "I've been a good man all my life. I've been a good husband and a good father. I've never hurt anyone in my life. Please, God, let me win the lottery."

He looked for his name in the paper the next day, but it wasn't there. This time he got down on his knees and said, "God, why did you let me down? What do you have to lose? Please let me win the lottery."

Suddenly, a deep voice boomed down from the heavens, "Do us both a favor. Buy _____!"
Clue: What is the one absolute prerequisite for winning the lottery?

68) A diplomat in Rome was commonly known to drink too much at official functions. At the reception for a foreign dignitary, he had started drinking long before the affair began.

As the formal evening began, the orchestra struck up a tune just as a vision in white swept by him toward the receiving line. With a gallant bow he whispered, "Lovely creature dressed in white, waltz with me this summer night."

The other stopped, looked at him and said, "No, I won't dance with you, and I'll give you three good reasons why. First, you are intoxicated. Second, this is not a waltz; it's the Italian National Anthem. And third, I am _____."
Clue: Who is the most famous person in Rome?

69) A terrible brush fire starts in a field near the high school, so the principal calls the volunteer fire department. Soon, a 40-year-old fire truck comes barreling by the gathering crowd, its sirens blowing and the bell ringing. It pulls off the main road and without even slowing down, heads directly into the center of the burning field. Fifteen volunteers jump off the truck with shovels and sand and hoses, and they gain control of the fire within a mater of minutes.

The crowd applauds them loudly, and a local reporter walks over to the soot-blackened chief and says, "Cap'n Donnelson, that was the bravest thing I ever saw. Protecting the high school by driving right into the center of the blaze and not even considering your own safety. Could you say a few words for people to read in tomorrow's paper?"

"Yes," said the chief. "Tell 'em to vote us the funds to _____ that damn truck!"

Clue: If they really hadn't planned on driving into the center of the blaze, what problem with the truck might have caused them to wind up there?

70) A good looking man walks into a bar in which four divorced women have gotten together for a drink. One of the ladies says, "Hi, I never saw you here before."

"No, it's my first time here."

"New in town?"

"Yes, I just got out of prison after 25 years."

"Prison? How did you wind up in prison?"

"Well, I got mad at my wife one night and killed her with a hammer. Then I dismembered her body with a chain saw and put her in a dumpster."

"Girls, he's _____!"

Clue: The woman's reaction is just the opposite of what you'd expect, given his past.

71) Two (name any group you want to victimize) who were recent converts to Christianity arrive together at the Pearly Gates.

"We're running a little late today," says St. Peter, "so I'll ask each of you just one question. Tell me," he asks the first man, "why do we have Easter?"

"That's easy," he answers. "It's the day Jesus was born."

"I'm afraid not," says St. Peter. "I can't let you in."

Then he turns to the second man and asks, "Do you know why we have Easter?"

"Certainly, that's the day that Jesus divided the Red Sea."

"I'm sorry," says St. Peter, "that's not good enough."

Finally he turns to the last man and asks, "And you. Do you know why we have Easter?"

He hesitates, but says, "Easter is the day Jesus was reborn."

"Excellent. Please continue."

"He was in the grave for three days."

"Very good. And then?"

"Well, after three days he saw his _____, and that meant they would have _____."

Clue: February.

72) Two French Canadians, Luc and Andre, hired a bush pilot to take them by seaplane out into the wilderness to go moose hunting. They flew in at sunrise and were to be picked up at sunset. All went well on the way in, but when the pilot returned, he found Luc and Andre with two large moose.

"You'll have to leave one of those moose behind," said the pilot, "the plane wouldn't get off the ground."

"Mais, no!" said Luc. "Last year a pilot take us out een same plane weeth two moose."

"Hmm," said the pilot, "I'm the best there is, so if another pilot did it last year, I can do it now. OK. load 'em up!"

So, they loaded both moose, all the gear, and Luc and Andre into the little plane. The plane roared across the lake struggling to lift off. It barely cleared the trees at the far side of the lake, but then stopped climbing. The pilot found a little clearing, and crash landed. Andre looked around; no one was hurt. "Well, Luc, how'd we do?" he asked.

"Preetty good," said Luc, looking around to get his bearings. "We got _____ than last year."
Clue: Luc didn't really say they got out successfully last year. What absurd way of thinking would lead them to be happy with how far they got before crashing?

73) A prominent biogeneticist is conducting research on the similarities between primates and humans. After a decade of careful preparation, he is preparing for his most daring experiment: the mating of a human with a gorilla.

He selects the perfect young gorilla and then advertises in the New York Times to find the perfect human partner: "Wanted: Single white male, age 25-30, with a Master's degree, non-smoker, loves animals, to impregnate a female gorilla. Stipend: $500."

He receives over a hundred responses and asks all of them to complete a lengthy questionnaire. Finally, he finds one who is the perfect mate. He says to him, "The job is yours, are you free to start Monday?"

"Just a minute," says the selected man. "I have a few conditions of my own. First of all, there'll be no kissing on the lips. Second, if there are any offspring, they must be raised in my own faith. And finally, could we wait a couple of weeks until I have a chance to raise the _____?"
Clue: He really wants to do this, and he misinterpreted the word "stipend."

74) The American Bar Association held their convention in Chicago, and three attorneys were sightseeing at the Sears Tower. As they stepped out on the observation deck, they were greeted by a mild mannered man standing on the very edge of the railing. "Hi!" he shouted. "Are you all lawyers from the convention?"

"Yes," said one. "Now get down from there before you fall."

"Oh, don't worry, you can't get hurt falling from here."

"Oh, is that so?"

"Yes, they've installed giant fans three floors down. If you fall from here, it triggers the fans, and they blow you right back up, safe and sound."

"That's absurd."

"Watch!" said the man, falling back over the rail. They rushed over to the edge, and sure enough, there was a giant "SWOOSH!" and he was blown safely right back up to the roof.

"It's great fun," he said. "You should try it."

So the three lawyers climbed up on the edge, linked arms, and jumped. Down they fell three floors, and nothing happened! They zoomed past the 90th, 60th, 40th, 10th ... and SPLAAATT!

Two cops sadly viewed the sidewalk. "More lawyers?" said the first. "Yes," said the other, shaking his fist up toward the sky. "That damned _____ hates them!"

Clue: Who is the one (fictional) person who could achieve the feat of being blown back up to the roof?

75) An Amish farmer in Pennsylvania was driving along in a buggy when he was hit by a car and permanently injured. He sued for damages, and was being questioned by an attorney representing the insurance company. "Is it true that right after the accident you told the state trooper that you never felt better in your life?" asked the attorney.

"I did," said the farmer.

"No further questions."

The mediator asked the farmer to explain the circumstances that led up to that statement.

"Well," said the farmer, "I was lying there in the road with my horse and dog when the trooper came up. He saw my horse writhing in pain and went over and shot him. Then he saw how badly hurt my dog was, and he shot him. Then he walked over to me and said, 'How're you feeling?' I said,

' _____.' "

Clue: No clue is necessary here.

76) Young Paddy O'Grady left Ireland for New York and made a fortune in the construction business. Then he went home and married a girl from the village he grew up in and brought her back to New York to live in a 30th floor penthouse. "All I ask," said Paddy, "is that you keep it like you kept your father's house back home."

"I will," she said. And later that day, she disappeared.

Paddy was very upset and called in both the police and private investigators to look for her. Four days later, she walked through the front door. "Thank God!" he cried. "But where have you been?"

"Washing _____."

Clue: What job that she might have had at home would take days to do in her new home?

77) A mail carrier is driving up to a farm, and is startled to see a farmer lifting a large pig up to the branch of an apple tree. He watches in amazement as the pig bites an apple off the tree, and then the farmer puts him down. The procedure is repeated with several pigs. Finally, the salesman can no longer restrain himself. "Excuse me," says the mail carrier, "but wouldn't it be easier to pick the apples yourself and let the pigs eat them off the ground?"

"Might be," says the farmer, "but what would be the advantage of that?"

"Well, for one thing," says the mail carrier, "it would save a lot of time."

"Could be," says the farmer, "but what's time to a _____?"

Clue: Remember, it's not what you expect. The farmer is confused about whose time the mail carrier is trying to save.

78) "Do you know what day today is?" a woman asked her husband at breakfast.

"Of course I do!" he answered.

In fact, he had no idea, but felt that he should know. He spent the entire day trying to figure it out. Could it be her birthday? No. Their wedding anniversary? No. Something about the children? No. The anniversary of their first date? The day he proposed? What could it possibly be?

He decided that he could take no chances, so he came home that night with flowers, champagne, and diamond ear rings.

"Well, did I remember today?" he asked with a smile?

"You certainly did," she replied. "It's the happiest _____ I've ever had."

Clue: It wouldn't be a joke if it were a date that really was significant.

79) During the early days of Glasnost, the KGB wanted some favorable publicity, so they conducted their own investigation of the attempt to assassinate the Pope in St. Peter's Square. They interviewed dozens of people, examined thousands of photos, and poured over hours of videotapes. Finally, they announced their findings: "The Pope _____."

Clue: This is a nonsensical conclusion. Think self-defense by the assassin.

80) Back in the 1950s, a train was speeding across the countryside during a rainstorm. The engineer didn't know that the rains had caused a torrent of water to roar down from the hills and destroy the bridge they were rapidly approaching.

A woman driving by spotted the washed-out railroad bridge. She knew she had to do something to stop the train that would soon be coming around the bend. She had no flashlight, no lantern. She had nothing but a clothespin. As the train approached in the distance, she rushed over to the tracks and held the clothespin up above her head. The white clothespin stood out sharply in the engine's brilliant light. The engineer

spotted it and immediately slammed on the breaks,
screeching to a stop 30 feet from disaster.

So, the question is, how did the engineer realize what
the woman was trying to tell her?

Well, everyone knows that a clothespin in the air
means, "_____ on the line."

Clue: Find a word linking what clothespins are
normally used for to what happened to the bridge.

81) A man looking for an apartment in New York was
walking along the East River when he suddenly heard
a man in the river crying for help. "Where do you
live?" cried the would-be rescuer. The drowning man
shouted his address and the "rescuer" rushed to his a-
partment to claim it.

"It's already rented," said the landlord.

"It can't be!" cried the other. "I just left the current
occupant drowning in the East River. Who could have
gotten here before me?"

"The guy who _____."

Clue: How did the occupant wind up in the river to
begin with? How desperate do people get when
they're trying to find an apartment?

82) In the early 1980s, an American manufacturer was
showing his farm equipment factory to a potential
customer from East Germany. At noon, the lunch
whistle blows, and two thousand men and women stop
work and leave the building.

"Your workers, they're all escaping!" cries the
visitor.

"Don't worry, they'll be back," says the American. And sure enough, the whistle blows again at 1 o'clock, and everyone heads back to their jobs.

After completing the tour of the factory, the manufacturer asks his guest, "Well, which of our products do you think you'd like to order?"

"Forget the farm equipment," says the East German. "What's the price of _____?"

Clue: What problem did Soviet-bloc countries often have with their workers?

83) A preacher was going on and on and on during his sermon, when a man suddenly got up and started to leave. "Where are you going?" asked the preacher.

"To get a haircut," said the man.

"Well why didn't you get a haircut before you came in here?"

The man answered, "Because I _____."

Clue: It was a very long sermon.

84) A politician storms into his speech writer's office: "That speech you wrote for me was terrible! It was too long! The first half was fine, but the second half was so boring that most of the audience got up and walked out on me!"

The speech writer says, "I gave you _____ that speech."

Clue: In fact, the speech the politician gave was exactly twice as long as it should have been. What would explain the entire second half being boring?

85) During a big fire in Yellowstone National Park in the 1980s, a photographer was assigned to get

photographs of the blaze. He arranged for a small plane at a local airport to take him up to get the photos. He arrived at the airport, and found a Cessina waiting near the gate with its motor running. He jumped in with all his equipment and shouted, "Ok, let's go!"

The pilot took the plane out to the end of the runway, and they were up in a matter of minutes.

"Fly over the park," said the photographer, "and make a few low level passes."

"Why?" asked the pilot.

"Because I'm going to take pictures!" he snapped. "I'm a photographer, and photographers take pictures!"

After a few moments of silence, the pilot said, "You mean you're not _____?"

Clue: Neither person is who the other thinks he is.

86) An old recluse loved his cat so much that he tried to teach it to talk. "Then I won't have to bother with humans at all," he said.

He tried every technique he could think of to train it to talk. First he tried food he thought the cat would love, canned salmon and canaries. The cat was delighted, but never learned to talk. One day it occurred to him to feed his talkative parrot to the cat. He cooked the parrot in butter, and served it to the cat on a bed of catnip. The cat loved it. He licked the plate clean, and then—incredibly—suddenly turned to his master and shouted, "Look out!"

The recluse didn't move, and the chandelier came crashing down on his head, killing him instantly. The cat just shook his head and said, "He spends two years

getting me to talk, and then the dummy doesn't
_____."

Clue: No clue necessary.

87) Three lovely daughters approach their father to get
his permission to marry. The father asks the first
daughter: "Who do you want to marry?"

"He's in the Tater family," she said. "He's an Idaho
Tater."

"Why the Idaho Tater is a fine tater. I'd welcome
him into our family."

"I want to marry a Tater too," said the second
daughter. "He's a Maine Tater."

"Another fine Tater," said the father. "I'd welcome
him as well. And who would you like to marry?" he
asked the third daughter.

"Peter Jennings."

"Peter Jennings? Why he's nothing but a
_____ tater!"

Clue: This is a pun. What kind of job does Peter
Jennings have?

88) Two opposing sects of the First Century Christian
Church struggle against each other for primary
influence and power: the Essenes and the Herds. The
Essenes believe that even children should qualify for
church membership, while the Herds believe that
membership should be restricted to adults. This may
be the origin of the familiar view that "Children should
be _____ but not _____."

Clue: Just play with the sound of the name of the two
groups.

89) A chimpanzee walks into a bar, orders a whiskey, and puts $10 on the bar. The bartender gets his whiskey and gives him his change—$2. And he says, "Pardon me for staring, but we don't get too many chimpanzees in here."

"Yeah," says the chimpanzee, "and at these _____ you won't see _____."

Clue: In this case, since the chimpanzee creates the strange circumstance, giving the normal response in this situation makes it funny.

90) A businessman who had been faithful to his wife throughout their 20-year marriage was in the midst of a mid-life crisis. While in another city on business, he spent an evening in a cocktail lounge and met a woman. They spent several hours chatting over drinks, and one thing led to another—and they wound up in his hotel room.

The next morning, she asked: "I hate to ask you this, but just to put my mind at ease, tell me, is there any chance that you might have AIDS?"

"None at all," he said. "I've been faithful to my wife for 20 years. I'm not sure why last night happened, but there's no chance at all that I have AIDS."

"Thank goodness," she said. "I wouldn't want to catch that _____."

Clue: It's the man who ought to be worried here, not the woman.

91) The Magna Carta was touring the U. S., and a man known for his slow-wit went to see it on his lunch hour. The guide was explaining that it was the source of English freedom and was signed by King John.

145

"When did he sign it?" the man asked.

"1215," said the guide.

"Damn!" said the man, looking at his watch,

"_____ _____!"

Clue: Link together the signing date, the time of day, and the fact that the man's not too bright.

92) Frank was a man who believed in the profound meaning of numbers. He was born May 5 and was about to turn 55 years old. He had five children, and lived at 555 East 55th St. He had earned $55,000 for the past 5 years at Saks Fifth Ave.

On his 55th birthday, Frank went to the track and was amazed to find a horse named "Cinco de Mayo" running in the fifth race. Five minutes before the race began, he went to the fifth window and bet $555 in five dollar bills on Cinco de Mayo. And sure enough, the horse finished _____.

Clue: Would you really expect him to win?

93) An international law firm is advertising for a paralegal who can type, answer the phone, take dictation, and speak more than one foreign language.

They are startled to discover that the first applicant is a black and white Scottish terrier. They are even more amazed to find that the dog can type 120 words per minute, knows shorthand, and has an excellent telephone voice.

The personnel manager stammers, "You're really extraordinary, but what about the foreign language requirement?"

"_____," replies the dog.

Clue: From a dog's point of view, what might count as a foreign language?

94) A tremendous rainstorm is flooding a small town. A farmer on the edge of town is forced to crawl out of his house and on to the roof as the water keeps rising. As he sits on the roof, a neighbor comes by in a rowboat and says, "Jump in, Hank."

"No thanks," says Hank, "I trust in the Lord. The Lord will save me."

Later that day, with the water still rising, a Coast Guard boat comes by and someone shouts, "You'd better come with us; the water's gonna keep on rising."

"No thanks. The Lord will take care of me."

The next day, it's still raining, and the man is forced to stand on top of the chimney with the water lapping at his feet. Then a helicopter flies over, lowers a ladder down to him, and someone shouts, "This is your last chance! Grab the ladder and let us take you out of here!"

"No thanks! I trust in the Lord! The Lord will save me!"

Well, the man eventually drowns. When he gets to the Pearly Gates, he says to St. Peter, "How could this happen? I had complete faith that the Lord would provide."

From nowhere, a thundering voice booms, "Look, I _____."

Clue: Assume that the Lord does provide, but not always in the way we may expect.

95) In the 1970s, there was a Russian worker who wanted to buy a washing machine. There weren't any

at the GUM (the Soviet state store), so he asked the store clerk how he could manage to get one.

"Go to the factory and buy one," said the clerk.

"That's where I work! They won't even talk to me."

"Then do what everyone else does," said the clerk. "Just steal the parts, take them home, and build it yourself."

"I've done that twice," said the worker, "but each time it turned out to be a _____."

Clue: What did the Soviet Union pour most of its money into prior to Glasnost? It wasn't washing machines.

96) A man was cruising along in his convertible on a warm, sunny day on a country road, when he suddenly noticed a chicken running along side. But this was no ordinary chicken. It had six legs and was running 40 MPH.

He accelerated, but the chicken kept up, running 50 MPH. He gunned it again. Sixty MPH, and the chicken was dead even with him. He pushed it to 70 MPH. The chicken was still there but was straining to keep up. Finally, at 80 mph, the chicken tired and fell behind.

The driver stopped for gas in the next town and described what had happened: "I saw the damnest thing a few miles back—a six-legged chicken running 70 MPH!"

"Oh," said the man, "it was probably from the Col. Sanders Experimental Chicken Farm."

"Of course!" said the driver, "a chicken with 6 drum sticks. Brilliant! They must be making a fortune."

"Not really," said the local, "I understand they
haven't _____ yet."
Clue: If they're that fast, what problem might it pose?

97) Sister Lucretia lives in a very strict convent where
the nuns have taken a vow of silence. They can speak
only two words every year. After the first year, she
goes to the Mother Superior and says, "Bed hard."

A year later, she again meets with the Mother
Superior: "Food bad," she says.

Yet another year goes by, and it's time for another
meeting with the Mother Superior. This time, she's so
unhappy that she blurts out, "I quit!"

"It doesn't surprise me," comes the reply. "Ever
since you got here, _____."
Clue: What has she done at every opportunity?

98) Sherlock Holmes and Dr. Watson go on a camping
trip. They put up their tent, fix a good dinner, share a
fine bottle of wine and then retire for the evening.
Some hours later, Holmes wakes up, nudges his friend
and says, "Watson, open your eyes and tell me what
you see."

"I see millions and millions of stars, Holmes," says
Watson.

"And what do you deduce from that?" asks Holmes.

Watson ponders this and then says, "Well,
astronomically, it tells me there are millions of
galaxies and potentially billions of planets.
Astrologically, I observe that Saturn is in Leo.
Horologically, I deduce that the time is about 3 a.m.
Meteorologically, I predict that we will have a
beautiful day tomorrow. Theologically, I can see that

God is all powerful and that we are a small, insignificant part of the universe. What does it tell you Holmes?"

Holmes lies silent for a moment and then says, "Watson, you idiot! Someone _____!"
Clue: How is it possible that they can see the stars?

99) Two young members of the southern gentry (one from Mississippi and the other from Texas) were sitting on a front porch swing at a southern Mississippi plantation house. The lady from Mississippi said, "When my first child was born, my husband built this beautiful mansion for me.

The Texas lady commented, "Well isn't that nice?"

The Mississippian continued, "When my second child was born, my husband bought me that Mercedes convertible over there."

"Well isn't that nice?" repeated the Texan.

The first woman went on, "Then when my third child was born, my husband bought me this exquisite diamond bracelet."

Yet again, the Texas lady smiled and said, "Well isn't that nice?"

The Mississippi lady then asked what the Texan's husband did for her when she had her first child.

The Texas lady said, "He sent me to charm school."

"Charm school!" the first lady cried, "Land sakes child, what on earth for?"

The Texas lady answered, "So that instead of _____, I _____ 'Well isn't that nice?'"
Clue: Fill in the second blank with "learned to say."

Extra Clue: She really is being polite. What if she said what she'd really like to say?

100) Miss Kline was grotesquely overweight, so her doctor finally prescribed a strict regimen, telling her it was the only way to avoid serious health problems in the future. "I want you to eat normally for two days, but then skip a day, drinking only water. Repeat this three times, and by the time I see you next Thursday you'll have lost at least 6 pounds."

The patient promised to obey and showed up for the next appointment almost 20 pounds lighter. "Excellent progress," enthused the doctor, quite amazed. "And you lost all this weight by simply following my instructions?"

Miss Kline nodded. "But it wasn't easy doctor. On that third day, I thought I was going to die!"

"From hunger, eh?" said the doctor sympathetically.

"No, no," she explained, "from _____."

Clue: Look back at the doctor's instructions for the third day. She misinterpreted them.

101) A doctor was performing a complete physical, including a visual acuity test. He placed the patient twenty feet from the chart and began, "Cover your right eye with your hand." The patient read the 20/20 line perfectly.

"Now cover your left." Again, a flawless read.

"Now try it with both eyes." There was silence. He couldn't even read the large E on the top line. The doctor turned and was surprised to find the patient standing there with _____.

Clue: How did the patient interpret "both eyes?"

102) Two Scottish nuns from a secluded convent have just arrived in the USA, and one says to the other, "I hear that Americans actually eat dogs." Her companion says, "Odd, but if we're going to live here, we might as well do as they do."

After they land in New York, the soon spot a street hot dog vendor. They nod to each other, and walk over. "Two hot dogs, please," says one. The vendor wraps them in foil, and the nuns excitedly walk over to a bench and unwrap their "dogs." The first nun unwraps hers and just stares at it for a moment. She then leans over to the other nun and asks cautiously, "What _____?"

Clue: She wasn't prepared for the idea that it was processed meat put into that particular shape.

103) Billy Graham went to see the Pope in Rome. As he was ushered into the waiting room, he noticed a red phone. Later, while talking to His Holiness, he asked, "What's the red phone for?" "That's to talk to God," said the Pope. "Really!" said Reverend Graham, "How much does it cost?" "Well, it's $20,000 a minute, but it's well worth it," answered the Pope.

A few days later, Reverend Graham went to see the chief rabbi in Jerusalem. He noticed that the rabbi also had a red phone. "I don't suppose," inquired a startled Billy Graham, "that this phone is to talk to God?" "Why yes it is," came the reply. "And how much does it cost?" "Oh, about 20 cents a minute," shrugged the rabbi. "Why is it so cheap?" Billy asked. "The Pope has a phone like that, and it costs $20,000 a minute!" "Well," grinned the rabbi, "from here, it's _____."

Clue: Where was Jesus born? What general principal used to apply to the cost of phone calls?
Extra Clue: Distance.

104) A strong young man at a construction site was bragging that he could outdo anyone in a feat of strength. He made a special effort to poke fun at one of the older workmen. After a while, the older worker had had enough. "Why don't you put your money where your mouth is?" he said. "I'll bet you a week's wages that I can haul something in a wheelbarrow over to that building, and you won't be able to wheel it back."

"You're on, old man," the braggart answered. "Let's see what you've got." The older man reached out and grabbed the wheelbarrow by the handles. Then nodding to the young man he said, "All right,
_____."

Clue: There's no real joke here. It's just clever thinking on the older man's part. There may be only one thing the young man could never carry, no matter how strong he is.

105) The "head" doctors in an insane asylum decide that one of their patients appears to be well enough to leave the asylum. So they take him to the movies as a kind of test. When they get to the theater, they see "Wet paint" signs pointing at the wooded chairs in the last 10 rows. The doctors just go to the row in front of those and sit down, but the patient grabs a newspaper and puts it down on one of the painted seats first and then sits down. The doctors look at each other with a sense of elation, because they think he really is in

better touch with reality now. So they ask him, "Why did you put that newspaper down first?" He answers, so I'd be _____ and have a _____ view."
Clue: His answer makes it clear he's note ready for the real world. What might a short person do in a crowded theater?

106) A woman walks into a bank in New York City and asks for the loan officer. She says she is going to Europe on business for two weeks and needs to borrow $5,000. The bank officer says the bank will need some kind of security for such a loan, so she hands over the keys to her Rolls Royce parked on the street in front of the bank. Everything checks out, and the bank agrees to accept the car as collateral for the loan. So she takes the car to the bank's underground garage and parks it there.

Two weeks later, the woman returns, repays the loan and the interest, which comes to about $30. The loan officer says, "We're very happy to have your business, but we're a little puzzled. While you were out, we checked you out and discovered that you have excellent financial holdings. What puzzles us is, why would you bother to borrow $5,000?"

The woman answered, "Where else in New York City can I _____ for _____ for _____?"
Clue: She didn't need the loan, but she's a real miser when it comes to spending money.

107) A Jewish man moves into a Catholic neighborhood. Every Friday he drives the Catholics crazy, because he loves to grill a steak on his back deck at the end of the week. The Catholics have to eat

fish and can't take the wonderful smell of grilled steak wafting through the neighborhood. So they decide to make a serious effort to convert him to Catholicism. After weeks of pleading and threats, they finally succeed. They take him to a priest who sprinkles holy water on him and says, "You were born a Jew, you were raised a Jew, and now you are a Catholic."

The rest of the week, all the Catholics were ecstatic. No more delicious, but maddening, smells of barbecued steak every Friday evening. But the very next Friday evening, there was that same familiar smell of grilled steak wafting through the neighborhood. Several Catholics rushed over to his house to remind him of his new diet. They arrive just in time to see him standing over the grill saying, "You were _____, you were _____, and now _____."

Clue: The priest's use of holy water.

108) A wife and her husband were having a dinner party for some important guests. She was very excited about this and wanted everything to be perfect. At the last minute, she realized that she didn't have the snails she wanted to serve, so she asked her husband to run down to the beach with the bucket and gather some snails.

He grudgingly agreed and headed down to the beach. As he picked up the snails, a beautiful woman walking on the beach stopped to chat with him about what he was doing. As they continued to talk, she became more and more friendly, finally inviting him to come for a swim with her. As she removed her top and shorts, he found it impossible to say no. Before he knew what had happened, he had spent a full hour frolicking playfully in the ocean.

When he realized the time, he quickly grabbed the snail pail and ran back to his apartment. He was in such a hurry running up the steps to his apartment that he dropped the bucket, and snails spilled all the way down the stairs. The door opened at that moment, with his angry wife wondering where he had been. He looked at the snails, looked up at her, then looked back at the snails and said, "Come on _____."
Clue: He's desperate for an excuse to explain his lateness. *Extra Clue*: Snails don't move very quickly.

109) A minister dies and is waiting in line at the Pearly Gates. Just in front of him is a guy who's dressed in sunglasses, a loud shirt, a leather jacket and jeans. St. Peter asks him, "Who are you, so that I may know whether you are to be admitted into Heaven?" He says, "I'm Joe Thomas, taxi driver from Noo Yawk City." St. Peter checks his list, smiles and says, "Take this silken robe and golden staff and enter the kingdom of Heaven."

The minister comes up next and stands proudly and says, "I'm Anthony Conrad, pastor of Saint Ann's Church for the past 35 years." St. Peter checks his list and says to the minister, "Take this cotton robe and wooden staff and enter the kingdom of Heaven."

"Now just a minute," says the minister. "That man was a taxi driver, and he gets a silken robe and golden staff. How can that be?" "Up here," says St. Peter, "we go by results. While he drove, people _____; while you preached, people _____."

Clue: The taxi driver scared people with his driving (so what did they do?). What do people often do in church when a preacher is not very dynamic in his/her delivery?

110) A symphony orchestra is performing Beethoven's Ninth. There's a long passage in this piece, about 20 minutes, during which the bass violinists have nothing to do. Rather than just sit there for 20 minutes, some of the bassists decide to sneak offstage and go to the bar next door for a quick beer.

   After slamming several beers in quick succession, one of them checks his watch and says, "Hey! We need to get back!" "No need to panic," says his colleague. "I thought we might need some extra time, so I tied the last few pages of the conductor's score together with a string. It'll take him a few minutes to get it untangled."

   A few moments later, they stagger back to the concert hall and take their places in the orchestra. About this time, a member of the audience notices the string around the pages, and says to her companion, "Well of course! Don't you see? It's the bottom of the _____, the score is _____, and the bassists are _____."

Clue: It's a baseball analogy. This would make for an exciting end of the game.

111) Two nuns are ordered to paint a room in the convent, and the last instruction of the Mother Superior is that they must not get even one drop of paint on their habits. After conferring about this a

while, the two nuns decide to lock the door of the room, strip off their habits, and paint in the nude.

In the middle of their project, they hear a knock at the door. "Who is it?" they ask. "Blind man," replies a voice on the other side of the door. The two nuns look at each other and shrug, deciding that no harm can come from letting a blind man into the room. So they open the door.

"Very nice," says the man. "Just where would you like me to _____?"

Clue: Focus on other meanings of the word "blind."

112) A teenager had just gotten his driver's license. He asked his father, who was a minister, if they could discuss his use of the car. His father said, "I'll make a deal with you. You bring your grades up, study your *Bible* more, and get your hair cut, and then we'll talk about it."

A month later, the boy came back to his father, who said, "Son, I'm real proud of you. You've brought your grades up, and you've studied your *Bible* diligently, but you didn't get your hair cut!"

The boy thought about it a minute and said, "You know dad, I've been thinking about that. Did you know that Moses, Noah and Jesus all had long hair?" His father replied, "Yes, and they _____ everywhere they went."

Clue: How can the father use what the boy said to support his initial rule? How did Jesus get from one place to another?

113) A priest is called away for an emergency. Not wanting to leave the confessional unattended, he calls

a rabbi friend from across the street and asks him to cover for him. Since the rabbi doesn't know how to do this, he just watches the priest for a while. A woman soon comes to the confessional and says, "Father forgive me for I have sinned. I committed adultery." The priest asks, "How many times?" and she says "Three times." The priest says, "Say two Hail Marys, put $5 in the box, and sin no more."

A few minutes later, a man also comes by and says, "Father forgive me for I have sinned." "What did you do?" "I committed adultery." "How many times?" "Three times." "Say two Hail Marys, put $5 in the box, and sin no more."

The rabbi says he thinks he's got it, so the priest leaves. A few minutes later, another woman enters and says, "Father forgive me for I have sinned." "What did you do?" "I committed adultery." "How many times?" "Once." And the rabbi says, "Go do it two more times. We have a special this week, _____."

Clue: The rabbi has focused on the wrong point here. What did the first two confessions have in common?

114) A Native American Chief on a Sioux reservation in South Dakota had a reputation for having a perfect memory. It was said that he remembered everything he ever did. A tourist tracked him down to see for himself how good his memory was. He walked up to him and said, "Howdy neighbor. I just wondered if you remembered what you had for breakfast on your 20th birthday." Without hesitation or a change of expression, he answered, "Eggs." The tourist went on his way, duly impressed.

Three years later, the same tourist was passing through and decided to look up the Native American with the perfect memory again. His wife (who had watched too many old westerns) told her husband that "Howdy neighbor" was hardly an appropriate way to address the man. Saying "how" would certainly be a more appropriate greeting. So when he spotted the chief, he walked over and said, "How." The chief said "_____."

Clue: The chief really did have perfect memory. Think back to the question asked three years earlier.

115)   A middle-aged priest invited a young priest over for dinner. During the meal, the young priest couldn't help noticing how attractive the live-in housekeeper was. During the meal, he began to wonder if there was more between his host and the housekeeper than met the eye. Reading the young priest's thoughts, the older priest volunteered, "I know what you must be thinking, but I assure you my relationship with my housekeeper is strictly professional."

About a week later, the housekeeper said, "Father, ever since that young priest came to dinner, I've been unable to find the beautiful silver gravy ladle. Could he have taken it?"

The priest said, "I'm sure he didn't, but I'll write him a letter just to be sure." His letter said, "Dear Father, I'm not saying you did take a gravy ladle from my house, and I'm not saying you did not take a gravy ladle. But the fact remains that one has been missing ever since you were here."

Several days later, he received a letter from the young priest which read, "Dear Father, I'm not saying you do sleep with your housekeeper, and I'm not saying that you do not sleep with your housekeeper. But the fact remains that if you were _____, you would have found the ladle by now."

Clue: He didn't take the ladle, but did put it somewhere in the host priest's house. Where could he put it to test his theory that the old priest was sleeping in the housekeeper's bed?

116) An 80-year-old man goes to a doctor for a check-up. The doctor tells him, "You're in terrific shape. There's nothing wrong with you. You'll probably have a long life. How long did your father live?"

The 80-year-old answers, "Did I say he was dead?"

The doctor can't believe it and asks, "How old was your grandfather when he died?" Again, the patient says, "Did I say he was dead?"

The doctor was astonished. He said, "You mean to tell me you're 80 years old and both your father and grandfather are alive?"

"Not only that," said the patient, "my grandfather is 126 years old and is getting married next week, 50 years after his first wife died."

The doctor said, "After 50 years of being single, why on earth does he want to get married?" The patient looked up at the doctor and said, "_____ _____?"

Clue: Look at the pattern of the patient's earlier remarks. Why do some couples get married even though they may not want to?

117) An after-dinner speaker is so rushed to get to his
engagement that when he arrives and sits down at the
head table, he realizes he's forgotten his false teeth.
The man next to him says, "No problem," and pulls a
pair of false teeth out of his pocket. "Try these," he
says.

The speaker tries them. "Too loose," he says. So the
man says, "I have another pair. Try these." "Too
tight." The man says, "I have one more pair. Try
them." "Ah," says the speaker, "they fit perfectly."
And with that, he eats his dinner and gives his talk
with no problem.

After the dinner meeting, the speaker goes over and
says, "I want to thank you for coming to my aid.
Where is your office? I've been looking for a good
dentist." The man replies, "I'm not a dentist. I'm
_____."

Clue: Where else might he get several pair of false
teeth? This will seem disgusting when you get it.

118) A cat dies and goes to Heaven. God meets him
at the gate and says, "You've been a good cat all these
years. If there's anything you'd like, all you have to
do is ask." The cat says, "Well, I lived all my life with
a poor family on a farm and had to sleep on hard wood
floors." God says, "Say no more," and a beautiful
fluffy pillow appears.

A few days later, 6 mice die and they go to Heaven.
God meets them at the gate with the same offer He
made the cat. The mice say, "We've had to run all our
lives. We've been chased by cats, dogs, even women
with brooms. If we could only have a pair of roller
skates, we wouldn't have to run anymore." God says,

"Say no more," and each mouse is instantly fitted with a pair of tiny roller skates.

A week later, God checks on how the cat is doing. He is sound asleep on his new pillow. God gently nudges him awake and asks, "How are you doing? Are you happy here?" The cat yawns and stretches and says, "Oh, I've never been happier. And those _____ you've been sending are the best."

Clue: What is a farm cat's favorite meal?
Extra Clue: Try rhyming with the word "meals."

119) A 90-year-old man is sitting on a park bench sobbing, when a young man walks by and asks him what's wrong. Through his tears, the man says he is in love with a woman half his age.

"What's wrong with that?" asks the young man.

"You don't understand. Every evening after she gets home from work, she makes one of my favorite meals, and then we make love. We do this day after day." The old man then breaks down and starts crying again.

The young man puts his arm around him and says, "I don't understand. It sounds like you have a great relationship. Why are you crying?"

The old man answers through his tears, "I _____ live."

Clue: He's 90 years old and senile.

120) Three lawyers and three engineers are traveling by train to a conference. At the station, the three lawyers each buy a ticket, but notice that the three engineers only buy a single ticket. One of the lawyers asks, "How are the three of you going to travel on only one ticket?"

Paul E. McGhee

"Watch and you'll see," answers one of the engineers. So they all board the train. While the lawyers each take a seat, the three engineers all cram into a restroom and close the door behind them. After the train leaves, the conductor soon comes around collecting tickets. He knocks on the bathroom door and says, "Ticket, please." The door opens just a crack, and a hand is extended with the ticket. The conductor takes it and moves on.

The lawyers see this and agree that it's pretty clever. So after the conference, they try the same thing and just buy a single ticket for the return trip. To their astonishment, the engineers don't buy a ticket at all. "How are you going to travel without even one ticket?" asks one of the perplexed lawyers. "Watch and you'll see," says one of the engineers.

When they all board the train, the three lawyers cram into one restroom, and the engineers all pile into another. The train departs, and shortly afterward one of the engineers leaves his restroom and walks over to the restroom where the lawyers are hiding. He knocks on the door and says, "_____."
Clue: They engineers have to get one ticket somewhere.

Answers to Stories and Longer Jokes

1) looking after my dog for a couple of hours
2) time … nature
3) I'll be damned
4) Goldberg
5) mouse ("bowl of milk" would also work here)
6) 2218 now
7) eat your spaghetti, you'll look just like that
8) ventriloquist
9) have a big glass of water
10) I was sick
11) don't have to get up in the morning
12) rink manager
13) wife's first husband
14) Catholic priest from a small parish
15) even swim
16) their ceiling light crashed to the floor
17) Pinocchio
18) stranger, what can I do for you (or any other line that indicates that Lenny has not recognized Sal)
19) executives it takes to make a pound of brains (you can replace "executives" with the name of any group you want to poke fun at)
20) Supplies
21) recognize you
22) sir
23) got caught
24) an acquittal

25) oom galla
26) relieving themselves on as many pigeons as they could find
27) rang a bell
28) dead ringer
29) rich
30) Don't forget
31) Fire
32) telling everybody
33) my money
34) 80 thousand dollars for the next three minutes
35) without a tie
36) Hair (hare) … wave
37) paw
38) your wife … you die
39) marked everything down 20%
40) talk
41) the guy who pushed me
42) arthritis
43) outrun you
44) De-de de de-de de-de …
45) $100
46) seeing-eye dog
47) rich
48) water
49) a motel
50) one portion
51) Do you think I should have said DiMaggio
52) lousy haircut
53) got up on the roof
54) an audience
55) in the attic
56) lousy conductor

57) light
58) Pepperidge Farms (or any other baker of bread)
59) Other men aren't as stingy as you
60) And she's only a 10
61) I THREW IT AWAY (note the significance of this being in capital letters)
62) the money ... the show ... get ready ... go
63) Go back to the bridge
64) are open
65) plane
66) Jewish
67) a ticket
68) the Pope
69) fix the brakes on
70) single
71) shadow ... six more weeks of winter
72) further
73) $500
74) Superman (again, note how easy it is to poke fun at any group you chose by substituting that group for lawyers)
75) I never felt better in my life
76) the steps ("windows" would also work)
77) pig
78) Ground Hog's Day
79) fired first
80) wash out
81) pushed him in
82) one of those whistles
83) I didn't need one then
84) two copies of
85) the instructor
86) listen

87) common (commentator)
88) seen (Essene) … heard (Herd)
89) prices … many more
90) again
91) It's 12:30. I just missed it! (Or any other remark which indicates that he interpreted 1215 to refer to the time of day.)
92) fifth
93) meow
94) sent two boats and a helicopter for you
95) tank (or any other kind of weapon)
96) caught one
97) all you've done is complain
98) stole our tent
99) saying, 'Who gives a damn (you can fill in your own other more extreme word here)' … learned to say
100) skipping
101) both eyes covered
102) part did you get
103) a local call
104) get in
105) higher … better
106) park my car … two weeks … 30 bucks
107) born a cow … raised a cow … you're a fish
108) guys, we're almost there
109) prayed … slept
110) ninth … tied … loaded
111) hang these blinds
112) walked
113) three for $5
114) Scrambled (or any other way of preparing eggs)
115) sleeping in your own bed

116) Did I say he wanted to
117) an undertaker
118) meals on wheels
119) forgot where I
120) Ticket, please

Paul E. McGhee

About the Author

Paul McGhee, Ph.D., is a psychologist, and is one of the world's foremost authorities on the benefits of building more humor into your life. He is internationally known for his own humor research, having spent 20 years conducting basic research on humor and laughter while teaching at the university level before becoming a professional speaker. He now works full time providing keynotes on humor in the workplace, the health and coping benefits of humor, and how adults can improve their humor skills. He is at the cutting edge of the current movement to bring a lighter attitude to the workplace.

For regular updates on humor and health and humor in the workplace, see his website, www.LaughterRemedy.com.

Dr. McGhee's work has been featured in *The New York Times, USA Today, Newsweek* and many other magazines. He has also been featured on the *Learning Channel, National Public Radio* and *PBS*. He has given talks on humor in 11 countries.

He is currently president of The Laughter Remedy, in Wilmington, Delaware. If you would like to arrange for a talk by Dr. McGhee for your organization, he may be contacted at:

The Laughter Remedy
302-478-7500
www.LaughterRemedy.com

Printed in the United States
16273LVS00003BA/79-560